Ovid's Metamorphoses

Selections

OVID'S
METAMORPHOSES
Selections

edited by
C. P. WATSON, M.A.
and
A. C. REYNELL, B.A.
line drawings by Diana Reynell

FABER AND FABER
LONDON · BOSTON

First published in 1968
by Faber and Faber Limited
3 Queen Square London WC1
First published in this edition 1972
Reprinted 1973 and 1979
Printed in Great Britain by
Butler & Tanner Ltd
Frome and London
All rights reserved

ISBN 0 571 10254 9 (paper covers)

Contents

Foreword   *page*   7

Introduction   9
  1. Metamorphosis and Myth   9
  2. The Augustan Poets   11
  3. Ovid as a Poet   12
  4. The Latin Hexameter   15

List of Abbreviations   19

The Tales
  1. The Golden Age (*Book I 80–112*)   22
  2. Apollo and Daphne (*Book I 502–67*)   30
  3. Phaethon (*Book II 150–70, 178–216, 227–
    34, 304–28*)   40
  4. The Daughters of Minyas *and* Pyramus
    and Thisbe (*Book IV 1–10, 31–166, 389–
    415*)   52
  5. Proserpina (*Book V 385–404, 438–45, 462–
    538, 564–71*)   70
  6. Philemon and Baucis (*Book VIII 624–50,
    660–724*)   86
  7. Orpheus and Eurydice (*Book X 1–63, 72–7*)   98
  8. Pygmalion (*Book X 247–97*)   108
  9. Midas (*Book XI 100–45, 172–93*)   116

Vocabulary   125

Foreword

This book is intended for the use of pupils in the year leading up to the Ordinary Level examination in G.C.E., or C.S.E., or for those who have passed O Level, but who wish, as part of their Sixth Form courses, to keep up or widen their acquaintance with what is best in Latin Literature. The introductions aim at placing Ovid and his stories in the tradition of Western literature and mythology. The Greek myths, their meanings and their origins, have fascinated the twentieth century; it seemed right, therefore, to stress in the introductions the kind of story with which we are concerned in each case, and how the story's theme has been treated in literature both before and after Ovid's time. Ovid himself is now coming to be recognized as a poet different from, but equal in rank to, poets like Lucretius and Virgil. The *Metamorphoses* by their brilliant telling of famous stories are capable of arousing wider interest than the obsolete physics of Lucretius, or Virgil's glorification of Roman imperialism. So the introductions also try to call attention to the sort of features in Ovid's art which make it so striking. All teachers will be able to think of further illustrations, both with regard to the story and to Ovid's literary qualities; so, probably, will their pupils. The introductions are intended only as a starting-point for discussion, which they may well provide by stimulating disagreement.

The notes are designed primarily to facilitate translation. Discussion of grammatical points has only been introduced when necessary for understanding the meaning of the Latin. The most important function of a commentary at this level is to minimize the barrier which the language builds between the mind of Ovid and that of his reader—without, of course, suggesting that a poet can be appreciated properly in any language other than his own. If the notes enable the reader to go a little faster in translating, our object will have been achieved.

The text used is that of the Loeb Edition, which is based on Ehwald. The spelling, except for the use of the letter j, has been brought into line with that recommended by Lewis and Short.

C. P. WATSON
A. C. REYNELL

Introduction

1. METAMORPHOSIS AND MYTH

The tales in this book come from a long work of Ovid's, in fifteen books, called the *Metamorphoses*. This is the plural of *metamorphosis*, a Greek word meaning 'change of form'. The *Metamorphoses* are a huge collection of stories, nearly all of which involve a change of form of some kind or other. Stories about human beings changing into beasts, birds, trees, stones, etc., have a history as long as human speech. Their origins, like the origins of myths and folk-tales in general, are too far back in time to be discoverable. But we may guess that they express a sense of the kinship of human life and human nature with the greater world of Nature. We can all of us think of examples of stories of human beings changing into something different—stories which may not, like Ovid's stories, come from Greece at all. We have heard of tales of men who change into werewolves at nightfall and back into human shape at daybreak; or of how the circles of standing stones which may be seen in various remote parts of the British Isles were once people, who danced on the sabbath and were punished for their impiety by being frozen into immobility. Here, clearly, we have a story made up in the Christian era about something which is pre-Christian. We are lucky if we can guess even as roughly as this about the origin of a Greek myth; but to remember such stories is the best possible way to get into the right frame of mind for reading the stories Ovid tells in the *Metamorphoses*.

Three of the stories included here tell of people changing into trees: Daphne, the sisters of Phaethon, and Philemon and Baucis. The daughters of Minyas turn into bats, the daughters of Achelous (in 'Proserpina') into birds with human faces, Ascalaphus (also in 'Proserpina') into an owl. But Ovid enjoys a good story which need not necessarily contain a metamorphosis: the stories of Phaethon, of the love of Pyramus and Thisbe, of the abduction of Proserpina by Pluto, of Orpheus' quest for his wife Eurydice, are there for their own sake; and the actual metamorphosis, more often than not, is incidental to the point of the story. Ovid uses metamorphoses as a connnecting thread. Also he liked an opportunity to exercise his ingenuity by working in as many metamorphoses as he could (see on 'The Daughters of Minyas' and 'Proserpina').

Ovid's *Metamorphoses* has been called the best book of stories in the world. But Ovid did not himself invent the stories, any more than Shakespeare invented his own plots. He drew from the store of Greek mythology—a store as valuable as any contribution which that most inventive of peoples has made to humanity. But it would be wrong to speak of even the Greeks as *inventing* these stories, since they turn up, with larger or smaller variations, all over the world. It would be truer to say that the Greeks *discovered* them within their own minds. Myths and folk-tales are one of man's ways—a more primitive way but not less fruitful than the developed philosophies and religions which come later— of expressing his discovery of himself and his place in the world, of the things he can do and the things he cannot do.

The tales we have included here range all the way from fundamental ones about the most basic facts, birth and death (see on 'Proserpina' and 'Orpheus and Eurydice'), to entertaining folk-tales like 'Midas'. Ovid, however, was not only little disposed to reverence himself, but was writing for sophisticated city-dwellers who were no more in touch with basic Nature than we are today. The state of literature in his time, and his particular kind of poetry, are the next things to be considered.

2. THE AUGUSTAN POETS

Ovid is the last of that group of Roman poets who are known as the 'Augustans' because they wrote during the period (27 B.C.—A.D. 14) when Augustus was First Citizen (*Princeps*). Many different kinds of writing were explored by these poets, but all except for satire were derived from Greek sources—from the Greek literature produced after the great age of Greece in what is known as the *Hellenistic* age (the last three centuries B.C.), as well as from the earlier literature of Homer, Hesiod, and the early Greek writers of lyric (Archilochus, Sappho, Alcaeus, Anacreon). The peak of Augustan literature was reached by Virgil (70—19 B.C.), in the *Aeneid*, an Epic poem modelled primarily on Homer as well as being in debt to Hellenistic writers. Before the *Aeneid*, Virgil had written his pastoral poems (the *Eclogues*) and his didactic farming poems (the *Georgics*), both derived from Hellenistic models (the latter also from Hesiod).

Horace (65-8 B.C.) was a writer of lyric poetry, for which he used the *metres* of the older Greek lyricists and the *themes* of the Hellenistic poets.

Propertius, a younger contemporary of Horace, wrote love elegies, and was actually nicknamed 'the Roman Callimachus' after the most famous of the Hellenistic poets.

Ovid (43 B.C.–A.D. 18) began his literary career by writing love poetry like Propertius, though the brilliantly executed *Amores* are totally devoid of the passion which gives Propertius his greatness. The famous *Ars Amatoria* ('The Art of Loving'), produced soon after 1 B.C., is a verse handbook for the young men of Rome on How To Get Your Girl.

His masterpiece, however, is universally acknowledged to be the *Metamorphoses*, in which he explored the vein of Comic Epic, hitherto untapped by any Roman poet, but derived from Hellenistic antecedents. In particular, the trick of combining short stories together to form a continuous whole had been popular with Hellenistic poets, and had been used by Callimachus in his longest and most famous work, the *Aetia* ('Causes'), concerned with myth, history, and ritual. But like the other great Roman poets, Ovid infused his own genius into this traditional form. Hellenistic influence explains Ovid's tendency to display his learning: such displays have been cut out in this selection, as for instance the long list of mountains which he inserts in a dramatic part of 'Phaethon'; but the tendency is apparent in the *names* he gives to people: he calls Midas, for example, the 'Berecyntian hero' (No. 9, l. 106), and who but a scholar could be expected to know that this is because Berecyntus was a mountain sacred to his mother Cybele? However, the Hellenistic poets were fascinated by obscure scholarship and took care that their readers knew it; and Ovid inherited this tendency like the other Augustan poets.

3. OVID AS A POET

Ovid was Shakespeare's favourite poet. Shakespeare knew the *Metamorphoses* well in the translation by Arthur Golding published in 1567. Nine-tenths of Shakespeare's knowledge of classical myth comes from Ovid, but the influence is far from being only external. Francis Meres wrote in 1578: 'As the soul of Euphorbus was thought to live in Pythagoras, so the witty soul of Ovid lives in mellifluous and honey-tongued Shakespeare'. As Ovid and the later Shakespeare were fascinated by myth, so Ovid and the early Shakespeare were fascinated by *wit*, i.e. a neat idea neatly expressed.

When Ovid wishes to express Thisbe's love for Pyramus and her determination to follow him to death, he hits on this way of expressing the idea (No. 4, l. 152f.):

> quique a me morte revelli
> heu sola poteras, poteris nec morte revelli.

We may clumsily translate this: 'You, whom Death alone could sever from me, not even Death shall have power to sever', and appreciate the neat *idea*: her love must lead to her suicide, now that her lover is dead. But the neatness of the actual Latin, with the identical line-endings, and the juxtaposed *poteras, poteris*, is the sort of craftsmanship which cannot be translated, and exactly the sort we find in Shakespeare's early plays, and which he recognized in Ovid: 'Ovidus Naso was the man; and why indeed *Naso* [Latin word for 'nose'], but for smelling out the odoriferous flowers of fancy, the jerks of invention' (*Love's Labour's Lost*).

Ovid's 'jerks of invention' are endless, and the reader of these tales, if he survives the struggle with the meaning of the Latin, will find enjoyment in discovering them for himself. But one aspect of Ovid's invention is worth stressing, if only because it is a feature that is thought to be lacking in Roman literature (though how it can, in view of Cicero's letters, Catullus, and Horace, is itself a puzzle). Ovid's work has the infinite addition of *humour*—not the screaming farce of music-hall and television, but the product of someone who gets amusement out of both fact and fiction. There is a conspicuous absence of ponderous solemnity about the *Metamorphoses* which some find a refreshing change from the super-serious Virgil, and which Shakespeare above all must have appreciated. Indeed the criticism of Ovid might be the opposite—that he is shallow and frivolous: the way he treats the sad tale of Pyramus and Thisbe is a case in point. Shakespeare was inspired by Ovid's comic treatment to write the farcical end of *A Midsummer Night's Dream*, but *Romeo and Juliet* shows that he could treat the same theme tragically. Ovid was constitutionally incapable of being serious for very long on end: often he seems deliberately to introduce things to make his readers smile or laugh, even at the gravest moments: after he has told of Pyramus' killing himself with his sword, he brings in a grotesque simile, comparing his spurting blood to water shooting out of a fissure in a flawed water-pipe. Such a simile at such a moment involves an element of bathos, which is appropriate to Ovid's comic account.

Ovid regularly enjoys himself over the metamorphoses themselves: nobody is expected to take seriously the metamorphosis of Philemon and Baucis, for example, who change into trees, from toe to top, so fast that they scarcely have time to utter a hurried goodbye before the bark swallows up their mouths (No. 6, 716–19). Apollo's operation on Midas' ears is also a source of fun (No. 9, 174–7). Arthur Golding translated:

Apollo could not suffer well his foolish ears to keepe
Theyre humaine shape, but drew them wyde, and made
    them long and deepe,
And filled them full of whytish heares, and made them
    downe too sag,
And through too much unstablenesse continually too
    wag.

The account of Philemon and Baucis is full of these touches of comic imagination, which enliven the narrative and cause a smile: as when they put a potsherd under one of the legs of their wobbly table to make it steady, or vainly attempt to catch their own goose (No. 6, 661–2 and 686–8). This is how Golding translated the second of these two incidents:

The Gander wyght of wing did make the slow old folke
    too spend
Theyre paynes in vayne, and mokt them long.

This makes a nice picture for the mind's eye. It is passages like these that show what Francis Meres meant when he spoke of Ovid's 'witty soul', and that explain Shakespeare's own love for him. What matters most about these passages from the *Metamorphoses* is Ovid's own genius. Some of the stories may have lost, in his hands, the grandeur and

impressiveness which they really possess, and which is pre-
served in other versions (we should think here of the
Homeric hymn's version of the tale of Proserpina, or of
Virgil's version of the tale of Orpheus and Eurydice, and
the reader of this book should find translations of these and
compare them with Ovid). But for charm, grace, wit, and
brilliant fancy, Ovid has no rival in Roman poetry, and
perhaps none in English except for Chaucer and Shakespeare.

4. THE LATIN HEXAMETER

Latin verse was written to be *heard*. It is thus essential
that it be read *aloud*, either before or after translating. No
treatment of a writer of verse can be adequate that does
not include reading him aloud.

By regular practice of this, the sound of the words and
rhythm will become familiar, and scansion will become
easy as readers learn to trust their ear.

The mechanics of the hexameter line are set out below,
and a mechanical method for scansion on paper is suggested, which may be used as a stop-gap until the ear is trained
by practice.

The line used by Ovid in the *Metamorphoses* is the
hexameter.

Hexameter is a Greek word meaning 'six-foot line' (*Hex* =
six; *metron* = foot). Below is a metrical scheme of the
hexameter line:

$$- \,\upsilon\,\upsilon \;\big|\; - \,\upsilon\,\upsilon \;\big|\; - \;\big\|\; \upsilon\,\upsilon \;\big|\; - \,\upsilon\,\upsilon \;\big|\; - \,\upsilon\,\upsilon \;\big|\; - \;\upsilon$$

Two short syllables ($\upsilon\,\upsilon$) are metrically equivalent to one
long syllable ($-$).

The metrical unit (foot) $-\;-$ is called a *spondee*.

The metrical unit $-\,\upsilon\,\upsilon$ (where the second long syllable
is 'resolved' into two short syllables) is called a *dactyl*.

From the above scheme it will be seen that any of the first four feet may be *either* a spondee *or* a dactyl, whereas the fifth foot *must* be a dactyl, and the sixth *must* be a spondee (except that its final syllable may be short).

VOWEL VALUES

i. Any vowel before two consonants will be long by *position* unless the second consonant is an 'r'.

ii. Any diphthong (combination of two vowel-sounds to form one syllable—ae, ai, au, ei, eu, oe, oi, ou) will be long.

iii. All five vowel sounds may have a long value or a short value:

a: *short*	sounds as in Fr.	'amour'	E.g. Latin	*a*mor
long	,,	,,	'father'	,,	f*a*ma
e: *short*	,,	,,	'bet'	,,	m*e*l
long	,,	,,	the 'a' in 'f*ai*r'	,,	v*e*r
i: *short*	,,	,,	'bit'	,,	*i*n
long	,,	,,	'feet'	,,	pr*i*mus
o: *short*	,,	,,	'hot'	,,	m*o*dus
long	,,	,,	'home'	,,	*o*tium
u: *short*	,,	,,	'put'	,,	*u*t
long	,,	,,	'hoot'	,,	t*u*tus

ELISION

A vowel (or a vowel followed by 'm') at the end of a Latin word is *elided* (i.e. eliminated for scansion purposes) if the word which follows begins with a vowel (or a vowel preceded by 'h').

E.g. in the first line of 'The Golden Age' (No. 1), the final *a* of *sata* will be elided before initial *e* of *est*: *sat(a) est*.

Similarly, in l. 94 of 'The Golden Age', the final *-um* of *peregrinum* will be elided before the initial *e* of *est*: *peregrin(um) est*.

Remember that initial 'h', and the 'u' of the combination 'qu', should be ignored for scansion purposes, and so should final 'm' if followed by a vowel at the beginning of the next word.

Let us take the first line of 'The Golden Age' as a specimen line to scan:

Aurea prima sata est aetas, quae vindice nullo

First we look to see if any syllables are *elided*: sat(a) est. Next, we *find the last two feet* by finding the last five syllables:

$$— ^5 \cup \cup \mid —^6—$$
$$\text{vindice} \mid \text{nūllō}$$

Then we can mark the first syllable of the line as *long* (it must be, whether the first foot is a spondee or a dactyl):

$$—$$

Aurea prima sat(a) est aetas, q(u)ae $\mid$ $—$ $^5 \cup \cup$ $\mid$ $—^6—$ vindice $\mid$ nullo

Next, we mark any syllables which are long by *position*:

ēst (before *st*)
aetās (before *sq*)

or because they are *diphthongs*:

$$— \qquad —$$
aurea, aetas, q(u)ae

Our line now looks like this:

$$\mid —^3— \mid — ^4 \quad — \mid —^5 \cup \cup \mid —^6—$$
Aurea prima sat(a) $\mid$ est aet $\mid$ as, q(u)ae $\mid$ vindice $\mid$ nullo

Now we know that the maximum number of syllables the first four feet could have (supposing they were all dactyls) is *twelve*: $— \cup \cup \mid — \cup \cup \mid — \cup \cup \mid — \cup \cup$ and that the minimum number (supposing they were all spondees) is *eight*: $— — \mid — — \mid — — \mid — —$

Let us therefore count the number of syllables in the four first feet.

There are *ten*.

We therefore know that *two* of the remaining feet must be dactyls and *two* must be spondees.

But we have already found the two spondees (since we can only have short syllables in *pairs* and never singly, an unidentified syllable between two long syllables must itself be long).

Therefore the remaining two feet must be dactyls.

$$—^1\ υυ\ \big|\ —\ υ^2\ υ$$

Therefore they must be: Aurea | prima sat(a).

We now have our line:

$—\ ^1υυ$	$—\ υ^2\ υ$	$—^3—$	$—\ ^4\ —$	$—\ ^5\ υ\ υ$	$—^6—$
Aurea	prima sat(a)	est aet	as, q(u)ae	vindice	nullo

It only remains to find the main *caesura* (or 'line pause' (lit. 'cut')), which always comes at a break between two words. $-\ -$

Look for it half-way through the *third* foot: *est aet*.

If it won't fit there, you'll find it *will* fit half-way through the *fourth* foot, and there will then be a *weak* caesura *between the two short syllables of the third foot* (which will in such a case always be a dactyl):

E.g., in the second line of 'The Golden Age':

	$—\ υ$	$υ$	$—$	$^4—$	
sponte sua sine	lege	fid	em	rect	umque colebat

POSTSCRIPT

You will be able to save a lot of time in working out if you *trust your ear*. You will very often *know* whether a particular vowel sound is long or short in sound: e.g., very few people think that the *i* in Latin *primus* sounds short (like English 'prim'); almost everyone knows that it sounds long (like English 'priest'). In such cases you can confidently mark it as such (not forgetting, of course, that short-sounding vowels can be made long by *position*).

Moreover, if your ear grows accustomed to the *sound* of Latin words by regular practice in reading, you will be able steadily to trust your ear more and more and gradually dispense with the mechanical system outlined above.

List of abbreviations used in notes and vocabulary

abl. = ablative
acc. = accusative
act. = active
adj. = adjective
adv. = adverb
comp. = comparative
cp. = compare
conj. = conjunction
dat. = dative
dep. = dependent
esp. = especially
f = feminine
foll. = following
gen. = genitive
inf. = infinitive
Innes = Mary Innes, translator of Penguin Classic
instr. = instrumental
intrans. = intransitive
l. = line

lit. = literally
m = masculine
n = neuter
nom. = nominative
obj. = object
pass. = passive
pf. = perfect
plur. = plural
prec. = preceding
prep. = preposition
pres. = present
pron. = pronoun
ptcpl. = participle
sc. = *sci*, understand
sing. = singular
subj. = subject
tr. = translate
trans. = transitive
usu. = usually
voc. = vocative

N.B. The letters f. and ff. following numerals referring to lines in the text:

E.g.: 7f. = line 7 and the following line.
7ff. = line 7 and the following line*s*.

1

The Golden Age

INTRODUCTION TO 'THE GOLDEN AGE'

This passage comes early in the first of the fifteen books of the *Metamorphoses*. It is the only one in this collection which does not tell a story, for the simple reason that it tells of a time before any stories could be told—a time of innocence and peace. There can be no stories about unchanging bliss.

According to the Greek poet Hesiod (? seventh century B.C.) the Golden Age had been followed by the Silver, the Bronze, and finally by the Iron Age in which men were still living. Each age was worse than the last, and in the Iron Age all the vices ran riot and the virtues abandoned the earth. This gloomy myth is followed by Ovid in the *Metamorphoses*, and was, in general, a favourite with the Augustan poets: Virgil, for example, when praising country folk in the *Georgics*, says that Justice (the last of the Immortals to desert the earth in the Iron Age) left her last footsteps among them.

The whole description is reminiscent of the opening of Genesis: 'And the Lord God planted a garden eastward in Eden; and there he put the man whom he had formed. And out of the ground made the Lord God to grow every tree that is pleasant to the sight, and good for food. . . . And a river went out of Eden to water the garden. . . . And the Lord God took the man, and put him into the garden of Eden to dress it and to keep it.' But Genesis tells of an abrupt fall, rather than of a gradual decline from bliss. All such legends of a paradise in the dim past reflect a feeling among men who 'grunt and sweat under a weary life', that life could be easier, and must surely once have been easier. It is the same longing that is expressed in folk-songs like 'Big Rock Candy Mountain'.

But there is also a feeling that agriculture is unnatural and does violence to Nature. As the American-Indian prophet said, 'It is a sin to wound our common mother by working at agriculture.' The words Ovid uses show that this thought was in his mind also: *immunis* and *intacta* in l. 101, *saucia* in l. 102. It is easy to understand the feeling that agriculture involves forcing man's will upon Nature instead of gratefully accepting her bounty.

89. *vindice nullo:* 'without any defender (of *fides* and *rectum*) being necessary'.

91f. *fixo aere:* 'on a bronze tablet', lit. 'a piece of bronze fixed (to a wall)'.

93. *ora:* 'the face'. Plural for sing., as frequently in Ovid. Cp. *mella* in l. 112.

   erant. sc. *mortales* as in l. 96.

94f. the subject is *pinus.*

96. *nullaque:* Sc. *litora.*

96. *norant* for *noverant*, from *nosco.*

98. Take both *directi* (straight) and *flexi* (curved) with *aeris.*

100. A peaceful-sounding line to describe a state of peace: it is a perfect example of a 'golden' line, with the two adjectives preceding, the verb in the middle, and the two nouns coming at the end. l. 112 is similar but less perfect.

101f. The subject is *Ipsa tellus*, 'the very earth herself'.

103. *cibis . . . creatis:* 'food produced with nobody forcing it', i.e. naturally.

106. *patula Iovis arbore*: I. e. the *aesculus*, tallest species of oak. probably for that reason sacred to Jupiter.

Book 1

1. THE GOLDEN AGE

In the Golden Age there was no law, crime, or punishment (89–93), no exploration (94–6), and no war (97–100); instead of tilling the ground men gathered fruit from bushes and trees (101–6); flowers and corn grew spontaneously and the land flowed with milk and honey (107–12).

Aurea prima sata est aetas, quae vindice nullo,
sponte sua, sine lege fidem rectumque colebat.   90
Poena metusque aberant, nec verba minantia fixo
aere legebantur, nec supplex turba timebat
iudicis ora sui, sed erant sine iudice tuti.
Nondum caesa suis, peregrinum ut viseret orbem,
montibus in liquidas pinus descenderat undas,   95
nullaque mortales praeter sua litora norant;
nondum praecipites cingebant oppida fossae,
non tuba directi, non aeris cornua flexi,
non galeae, non ensis erant: sine militis usu
mollia securae peragebant otia gentes.   100
Ipsa quoque immunis rastroque intacta nec ullis
saucia vomeribus per se dabat omnia tellus,
contentique cibis nullo cogente creatis
arbuteos fetus montanaque fraga legebant
cornaque et in duris haerentia mora rubetis   105
et quae deciderant patula Iovis arbore glandes.
Ver erat aeternum, placidique tepentibus auris

110. *nec renovatus = et non renovatus.* 'And the field, without being renewed (by ploughing) . . .'

mulcebant zephyri natos sine semine flores;
mox etiam fruges tellus inarata ferebat,
nec renovatus ager gravidis canebat aristis;   110
flumina iam lactis, iam flumina nectaris ibant,
flavaque de viridi stillabant ilice mella.

2

Apollo and Daphne

INTRODUCTION TO 'APOLLO AND DAPHNE'

This brilliantly humorous and irreverent piece is like something out of the world of comic opera, with Apollo in the
role of a frustrated Don Juan.

According to the version of the story which Ovid is
following, Daphne was the daughter of the river Peneus.
She was a follower of Artemis, goddess of hunting and
chastity; so she wanted to have nothing to do with men.
But the god Apollo, and Leucippus, son of Oinomaus, king
of Pisa (in Greece), were both in love with her. Leucippus
disguised himself as a woman in order to be near her, but
the jealous Apollo suggested to Daphne that she should
bathe with her companions, and this led to Leucippus
being discovered and consequently killed by them. But as
this story relates, Apollo's pursuit of her had no success
either.

The Greek word *Daphne* means a Bay Laurel (*Laurus
nobilis*), and as the end of this story makes clear, this tree
was sacred to Apollo. Another legend tells how the pine
tree was once a nymph called Pitys (this being the Greek
word for a pine tree), who was pursued by Pan and turned
into the tree that bears her name.

The character-sketch of Apollo is masterly: note his
naive snobbery (513f.), comparable to Don Giovanni's
scorn for *la gente plebea*, 'common folk', in Mozart's opera,
and the way he reels off a testimonial (515f.). Finally, when
traditional methods of courtship have had no result, he has
no more scruples than Don Giovanni about resorting to

force (530f.): he abruptly decides that he is not prepared to waste any more time.

The passage is full of inspired touches of comedy: Daphne's chastity is ice-cold to the last, even when she has become a tree (556), though she is gracious enough to acknowledge with a nod the honours Apollo bestows on her (566f.). There are also some good examples of Ovid's *wit* (see Introduction): see lines 519f., 522-4.

NOTES TO
'APOLLO AND DAPHNE'

503. *revocantis:* Sc. *Apollinis* (gen. of *Apollo*).

504. *Penei:* Voc. of *Peneis, -idis,* 'of Peneus'.

 hostis. nom., 'as an enemy', 'with hostile intent'.

506. *penna trepidante:* 'on fluttering wing'.

507. *hostes quaeque suos:* Sc. *fugit.*

508. *me miserum!* exclamatory acc., hard to render without making it sound silly. Innes tr. simply 'Alas'.

 ne cadas: ne with the subjunctive is a common form of prohibition in verse.

 laedi: inf. after *indigna,* lit. 'not deserving to be hurt'.

510. *moderatius:* 'slower'. But the word, like *inhibe* in the next line, contains the suggestion that Daphne, by running full tilt, is offending against maidenly decorum.

512. *cui placeas:* indirect question dependent on *inquire.* Lit. 'whom you please', and so 'who it is that loves you'.

515. *Delphica:* 'of Delphi', where Apollo's oracle was.

516. These are all places in and around Asia Minor famed in connexion with the worship of Apollo.

518. *patet:* the subj. is the relative clause *quod . . . estque.*

519. *Certa . . . est.* sc. *sagitta.* The first *nostra* is nom., the second comparative abl. Apollo was the god of archery, and he says here that though his aim is good, Cupid's is even better.

520. *vacuo.* i.e., free from love.

521. *Inventum . . . est.* tr. 'medicine is my discovery'.

522. *herbarum:* here 'healing herbs'.

523. *ei mihi:* lit. 'alas for me'.

 herbis: dat. of the agent with *sanabilis.*

524. Cp. 'he saved others, himself he cannot save'.

Book 1

2. APOLLO AND DAPHNE

As Daphne runs away, Apollo pursues her with wheedling words, stressing his pedigree and accomplishments (502–24).

Fugit ocior aura	502

illa levi neque ad haec revocantis verba resistit:
'Nympha, precor, Penei, mane! non insequor hostis;
nympha, mane! sic agna lupum, sic cerva leonem,   505
sic aquilam penna fugiunt trepidante columbae,
hostes quaeque suos: amor est mihi causa sequendi!
me miserum! ne prona cadas indignave laedi
crura notent sentes et sim tibi causa doloris!
aspera, qua properas, loca sunt: moderatius, oro,   510
curre fugamque inhibe, moderatius insequar ipse.
Cui placeas, inquire tamen: non incola montis,
non ego sum pastor, non hic armenta gregesque
horridus observo. Nescis, temeraria, nescis,
quem fugias, ideoque fugis: mihi Delphica tellus   515
et Claros et Tenedos Patareaque regia servit;
Iuppiter est genitor; per me, quod eritque fuitque
estque, patet; per me concordant caimina nervis.
Certa quidem nostra est, nostra tamen una sagitta
certior, in vacuo quae vulnera pectore fecit!   520
Inventum medicina meum est, opiferque per orbem
dicor, et herbarum subiecta potentia nobis.
Ei mihi, quod nullis amor est sanabilis herbis
nec prosunt domino, quae prosunt omnibus, artes!'

525. *Peneia:* this time from *Peneius -a -um,* but with the same meaning as in l. 504.
527. *visa decens:* tr. 'looking beautiful'.
   corpora: plur. for sing.
528. *obvia* and *adversas* both mean much the same: 'the wind *in her path* fluttered her garments *as it blew against them*'.
529. *levis:* stock epithet for *aura,* because air is so easily moved.
   retro dabat: tr. 'blew back'.
533–8. These lines contain a simile.
533. *canis Gallicus:* a greyhound.
535. *inhaesuro similis:* sc. *est.* lit., 'is like to one about to grasp (her)'.
   iam iam: tr. 'at any moment'.
537. *alter:* the hare.
538. *tangentiaque ora relinquit:* 'and escapes from the jaws which are (almost) touching her'.
542. *cervicibus:* plur. for sing., 'over her neck'.
545. *si flumina numen habetis:* 'if your streams have divine power'.
546. *qua:* instrumental abl. The antecedent is *figuram.*
   mutando: sc. *meam figuram.*
551. *pigris radicibus haeret:* 'is held fast with immovable roots'.
552. *remanet . . . illa:* lit. '(it, the *cacumen*) remains the one beauty in her'; tr. 'that is the sole remaining trace of her former beauty'.

On the point of being caught by Apollo, Daphne prays to her father, the river-god Peneus, to have her shape changed. She is promptly changed into a laurel tree (525–52).

Plura locuturum timido Peneia cursu   525
fugit cumque ipso verba imperfecta reliquit,
tum quoque visa decens; nudabant corpora venti,
obviaque adversas vibrabant flamina vestes,
et levis impulsos retro dabat aura capillos,
auctaque forma fuga est. Sed enim non sustinet ultra   530
perdere blanditias iuvenis deus, utque movebat
ipse Amor, admisso sequitur vestigia passu.
Ut canis in vacuo leporem cum Gallicus arvo
vidit, et hic praedam pedibus petit, ille salutem;
alter inhaesuro similis iam iamque tenere   535
sperat et extento stringit vestigia rostro,
alter in ambiguo est, an sit comprensus, et ipsis
morsibus eripitur tangentiaque ora relinquit:
sic deus et virgo est hic spe celer, illa timore.
Qui tamen insequitur pennis adiutus Amoris,   540
ocior est requiemque negat tergoque fugacis
imminet et crinem sparsum cervicibus afflat.
viribus absumptis expalluit illa citaeque
victa labore fugae spectans Peneidas undas
'Fer, Pater,' inquit, 'opem! Si flumina numen habetis,
qua nimium placui, mutando perde figuram!'
Vix prece finita torpor gravis occupat artus,
mollia cinguntur tenui praecordia libro,
in frondem crines, in ramos bracchia crescunt,   550
pes modo tam velox pigris radicibus haeret,
ora cacumen habet: remanet nitor unus in illa.

554. *sentit adhuc trepidare pectus:* 'he can feel the heart still beating fast'.

555. *ut membra:* 'as though they were limbs'.

558. *habebunt:* i.e., for adornment, decoration.

559. Sc. *nostra* with *coma* and *nostrae* with *citharae.*

560–5. A prophecy that the laurel shall be worn by victorious generals and shall watch over the portals of Augustus and the wreath of oak leaves upon them.

560. *Latiis* (adj.): strictly 'of Latium', but here equivalent to *Romanis.*

   Triumphum: 'Io Triumphe' was the slogan chanted by the crowds and victorious troops during Roman triumphal processions.

561. *Capitolia:* because at the end of the triumphal procession the victorious general ascended the Capitoline hill to Jupiter's temple.

562. *postibus Augustis:* i.e. the doors of the *domus Augusti* on the Palatine hill, which had a laurel tree in front of them.

563. *mediam quercum:* 'the oaken garland between'. This was the *corona civica,* the 'civic' oak wreath, conferred as a perpetual honour on Augustus in 27 B.C. It adorned the doors of his house thenceforward.

565. *perpetuos frondis honores:* lit., 'perpetual honours of foliage' and so 'the glory of perennial foliage'.

566. *factis modo:* 'just newly made'.

567. *ut caput:* see note on *ut membra,* l. 555.

The thwarted god vows to make her his own sacred tree, and mentions the privileges she will have (553-67).

Hanc quoque Phoebus amat positaque in stipite dextra
sentit adhuc trepidare novo sub cortice pectus
complexusque suis ramos ut membra lacertis   555
oscula dat ligno; refugit tamen oscula lignum.
Cui deus 'At, quoniam coniunx mea non potes esse,
arbor eris certe' dixit 'mea! semper habebunt
te coma, te citharae, te nostrae, laure, pharetrae;
tu ducibus Latiis aderis, cum laeta Triumphum   560
vox canet et visent longas Capitolia pompas;
postibus Augustis eadem fidissima custos
ante fores stabis mediamque tuebere quercum,
utque meum intonsis caput est iuvenale capillis,
tu quoque perpetuos semper gere frondis honores!'   565
Finierat Paean: factis modo laurea ramis
adnuit utque caput visa est agitasse cacumen.

3

Phaethon

INTRODUCTION TO 'PHAETHON'

Phaethon was the son of Clymene by Helios the Sun-God.
Taunted by his boyhood companion Epaphus, who said he
was not really the son of Helios at all, Phaethon begged
his mother for proof. She suggested that he should go and
ask Helios himself. So he travelled to the Sun-God's palace
in the far East, and Helios there told him that he was indeed his father, and promised to give him anything he
asked for. Phaethon then asked to be allowed to drive the
chariot of the Sun for one day. Despite his father's attempts
to dissuade him, he persisted in this request; and his father,
having promised, could not give an outright refusal. This
is the point in the story where this selection starts.

The rash promise of a gift which turns out to be disastrous
is a common folk-tale motif: we shall meet it again in the
Midas tale (No. 9). But the main point of the Phaethon
story is clearly a moral one—don't bite off more than you
can chew. The epitaph on Phaethon written by the water-
nymphs, MAGNIS EXCIDIT AUSIS ('he failed in a great en-
deavour'), makes the best of a bad job, but Phaethon's
conduct was in fact silly rather than heroic. The whole
story reminds us of Hilaire Belloc's 'Cautionary Tales for
Children'.

Ovid's telling of the story is uneven in quality. The description of Phaethon's state of mind—his joy when he
first gets into the car and grasps the reins (151f.), his terror
as he agonizedly turns his head back and forth, helplessly
wondering whether he has reached the 'point of no return'
(187ff.)—and the vividness in the account of the 'ghost-

train' sights he sees as he's whirled past the constellations, are among the best things in Ovid. But in the second half (where we have made extensive cuts) Ovid's wish to show off his learning gets the better of him: he cannot resist putting down the name of every mountain he can think of that ever occurred in classical myth, and saying that they all got burned, and then doing the same with the rivers and saying that they all got dried up. However, he finishes with a magnificent image (319–22) of Phaethon falling like a shooting-star, which took hold of Shakespeare: King Richard II, in a typical moment of self-dramatization, compares his own fall to that of Phaethon:

'Down, down I come; like glistering Phaethon,
wanting the manage of unruly jades.'

NOTES TO 'PHAETHON'

150. *ille:* Phaethon.
156. *Tethys:* a sea-goddess, mother of Clymene and there-fore grandmother of Phaethon.
157. *facta . . . copia:* lit., 'opportunity of the mighty heaven was made'; tr., 'the way through the mighty heaven lay open'.
158. *corripuere:* sc. *Solis equi* as subject.
   pedibus . . . motis: Tr. 'and galloping through the sky'.
160. *ortos . . . Euros:* 'the East winds that rise in those same quarters'.
161. *nec . . . possent:* lit., 'and not what they could have recognized'. Tr. 'and unfamiliar to . . .'
163. *utque:* introduces a simile likening the chariot to a ship tossed about at sea.
164. Tr. 'and move over the sea unsteadily, because they are too light'.
165f. *currus* is the subject of these two lines.
166. *inani:* sc. *currui.* The chariot was behaving just like an empty one.
167. *Quod:* i.e., the fact that the chariot was lighter.
168. *quo prius* (sc. *cucurrerunt*) : the antecedent to *quo* is *ordine.* Tr. 'in their regular course'.
169. *Ipse:* Phaethon.
169f. *qua flectat . . . qua sit:* indirect questions dependent on *scit.*
170. *imperet illis:* 'would he be able to control them (the horses)'.

Book 2

3. PHAETHON

Phaethon leaps into the chariot, and sets off (150–
60); but the horses, finding the chariot lighter than
usual, leave their usual course. Phaethon begins to
panic (161–70).

Occupat ille levem iuvenali corpore currum   150
statque super manibusque datas contingere habènas
gaudet et invito grates agit inde parenti.
  Interea volucres Pyrois et Eous et Aethon,
Solis equi, quartusque Phlegon hinnitibus auras
flammiferis implent pedibusque repagula pulsant.   155
Quae postquam Tethys, fatorum ignara nepotis,
reppulit et facta est immensi copia caeli,
corripuere viam pedibusque per aera motis
obstantes scindunt nebulas pennisque levati
praetereunt ortos isdem de partibus Euros.   160
Sed leve pondus erat nec quod cognoscere possent
Solis equi, solitaque iugum gravitate carebat;
utque labant curvae iusto sine pondere naves
perque mare instabiles nimia levitate feruntur,
sic onere assueto vacuus dat in aera saltus   165
succutiturque alte similisque est currus inani.
Quod simulac sensere, ruunt tritumque relinquunt
quadriiugi spatium nec quo prius ordine currunt.
Ipse pavet nec qua commissas flectat habenas
nec scit qua sit iter, nec, si sciat, imperet illis.   170

179. *penitus penitusque*: lit., 'completely and utterly'. The higher one is the farther one can see in every direction. Ph. was so high that the whole earth lay open to his vision. Tr. 'far and wide'.

181. lit., 'and darkness overwhelmed his eyes because of the excess of light'. In a word, he was dazzled.

183. *cognosse* = *cognovisse*, 'to have found out'.
    valuisse rogando: lit., 'to have got his way by asking'.

184. *Meropis*: '(the son) of Merops'. Merops was Clymene's husband, and the supposed father of Phaethon.
    ita fertur, ut: lit. 'he is carried along in like manner as . . .'

185. *cui*: dat. of disadvantage. The antecedent, as for *quam* in the next line, is *pinus*.
    victa: by the force of the wind.

186. *dis votisque*: Dat., lit. 'to the gods and to prayers', i.e. to superhuman dispensation.

187. *caeli*: partitive genitive after *multum*.

188. *animo . . . utrumque*: 'he makes a mental reckoning of each distance'.

189f. *modo . . . interdum* = modo . . . modo.

189. *quos . . . est*: the antecedent to *quos* is *occasus* in the next line. Lit. 'which it is not destiny for him to reach'.

190. *occasus, ortus*: sc. *solis*, i.e. west and east.

191. *quid agat*: indirect question dep. on *ignarus*.
    stupet: 'is paralyzed (with indecision)'.

193. *in vario caelo*: 'in the various (parts of the) sky'.

195. *ubi*: introduces the clause despite its postponed position. Tr. straight after *locus*.

196. *Scorpius*: the Scorpion, a zodiacal sign, *aliis Libra*, the Scales.
    flexis . . . lacertis: 'with his claws (lit. arms) curving out on both sides'. The clause apparently states in another way the fact already contained in the words *in geminos bracchia concavat arcus*.

197. *signorum*: 'signs (of the zodiac)'.

198f. The clause is introduced by *ut*(='when').

199. *vulnera*: obj. of *minitantem*.

200. *mentis inops*: 'out of his mind'.

201. *iacentia*: 'lying loose'. *tergum*: sc. *equorum*.

Lines 171–77 contain some rather tedious astro-
nomical details and are therefore omitted.
Phaethon's panic gets steadily worse, but he is unable to control the team (178–92); finally he drops
the reins and the horses run away madly, dashing
up into outer space, and then (206) plunging down
and setting the earth on fire (193–216).

Ut vero summo dispexit ab aethere terras
infelix Phaethon penitus penitusque patentis,
palluit et subito genua intremuere timore   180
suntque oculis tenebrae per tantum lumen obortae,
et iam mallet equos numquam tetigisse paternos,
iam cognosse genus piget et valuisse rogando,
iam Meropis dici cupiens ita fertur, ut acta
praecipiti pinus borea, cui victa remisit   185
frena suus rector, quam dis votisque reliquit.
Quid faciat? Multum caeli post terga relictum,
ante oculos plus est: animo metitur utrumque
et modo, quos illi fatum contingere non est,
prospicit occasus, interdum respicit ortus,   190
quidque agat ignarus stupet et nec frena remittit
nec retinere valet nec nomina novit equorum.
sparsa quoque in vario passim miracula caelo
vastarumque videt trepidus simulacra ferarum.
Est locus, in geminos ubi bracchia concavat arcus   195
Scorpius et cauda flexisque utrimque lacertis
porrigit in spatium signorum membra duorum:
hunc puer ut nigri madidum sudore veneni
vulnera curvata minitantem cuspide vidit,
mentis inops gelida formidine lora remisit;   200
quae postquam summum tetigere iacentia tergum,
exspatiantur equi nulloque inhibente per auras

(45)

202. *exspatiantur:* they had already done this in ll. 167f., but hadn't altered their whole *direction*, as 178ff. show.

204f. *altoque . . . stellis.* According to the cosmology made canonical by Aristotle, the Earth was enclosed within eight concentric spheres, the inmost being that of the moon (l. 208f.), and the outermost that of the fixed stars; outside all the others was the Empyrean—to which Ovid here refers as the *aether.*

208. *suis:* Comparative abl., sc. *equis.*

210. *ut quaeque altissima:* sc. *est.* Lit. 'as each (bit is) highest'. Tr. 'all the highest parts'.

211. *agit rimas:* 'breaks into cracks'.

212. *canescunt:* 'turn white', i.e. are burned to white ashes.

214. *parva queror:* lit. '(these are) small (disasters) I lament', i.e., worse ones follow.

230. *ore trahit:* i.e., he breathes in.

233. *quoque . . . sit:* indirect questions dep. on *nescit* in the foll. line.

ignotae regionis eunt, quaque impetus egit,
hac sine lege ruunt altoque sub aethere fixis
incursant stellis rapiuntque per avia currum   205
et modo summa petunt, modo per declive viasque
praecipites spatio terrae propiore feruntur,
inferiusque suis fraternos currere Luna
admiratur equos, ambustaque nubila fumant.
corripitur flammis, ut quaeque altissima, tellus   210
fissaque agit rimas et sucis aret ademptis;
pabula canescunt, cum frondibus uritur arbor,
materiamque suo praebet seges arida damno.
Parva queror: magnae pereunt cum moenibus urbes,
cumque suis totas populis incendia gentis   215
in cinerem vertunt; silvae cum montibus ardent.

> Here follows a long list of famous mountains which
> were burned (217–26, omitted).
> Phaethon is overcome by the heat (227–34).

Tum vero Phaethon cunctis e partibus orbem   227
aspicit accensum nec tantos sustinet aestus
ferventisque auras velut e fornace profunda
ore trahit currusque suos candescere sentit;   230
et neque iam cineres eiectatamque favillam
ferre potest calidoque involvitur undique fumo,
quoque eat aut ubi sit, picea caligine tectus
nescit et arbitrio volucrum raptatur equorum.

> After giving a long list of rivers which were dried up,
> Ovid tells how Jupiter hurls a thunderbolt which
> kills Phaethon and shatters the chariot (235–318,
> omitted). Phaethon falls into the River Po, and is
> buried by the river-nymphs (319–28).

320. *volvitur in praeceps:* 'is tumbled out headlong'.

321. *ut interdum:* 'just as every now and then . . .'

322. *cecidisse* depends on *videri*, which is inf. after *potuit*. It *looks* as though a star has fallen when we see a meteor track.

323. *quem:* Phaethon.

 diverso orbe: 'in a different part of the world'. Ph.'s homeland was, of course, Greece.

324. *Eridanus:* the river Po.

 ora: plur. for sing.

325. *Naiades Hesperiae:* lit. 'the Western nymphs', here the nymphs of one of the 'Western' rivers, the Po. Any place west of Greece was regarded as 'Western' for the purposes of Greek history and mythology.

 trifida flamma: of Jupiter's thunderbolt. The abl. is causal, constructed with *fumantia.*

326. *corpora:* plur. for sing.

327. *HIC. SITUS. EST.:* the regular formula on tombstones, usu. appearing as H.S.E. 'Here lies'.

328. *QUEM.:* connecting relative. The antecedent is *currus* (gen.) in the preceding line.

 TENUIT.: in normal script there would be a comma after this word.

 MAGNIS . . . AUSIS.: See introd. to this piece.

364. *Inde:* i.e., from the trees.

 sole: instrumental abl. with *rigescunt.*

366. *nuribus gestenda Latinis:* 'to be worn (as ornaments) by Roman brides'.

At Phaethon rutilos flamma populante capillos
volvitur in praeceps longoque per aera tractu   320
fertur, ut interdum de caelo stella sereno
etsi non cecidit, potuit cecidisse videri.
Quem procul a patria diverso maximus orbe
excipit Eridanus fumantiaque abluit ora.
Naides Hesperiae trifida fumantia flamma   325
corpora dant tumulo, signant quoque carmine saxum;
HIC.SITUS.EST.PHAETHON.CURRUS.AURIGA.PATERNI.
QUEM.SI.NON.TENUIT.MAGNIS.TAMEN.EXCIDIT.AUSIS.

> Phaethon's sisters came to mourn for him, and
> were turned into trees (329–63, omitted). Their
> tears thus became drops of amber (364–6).

Inde fluunt lacrimae, stillataque sole rigescunt
de ramis electra novis, quae lucidus amnis   365
excipit et nuribus mittit gestanda Latinis.

4

The Daughters of Minyas
including the tale of
Pyramus and Thisbe

INTRODUCTION TO
'THE DAUGHTERS OF MINYAS'

This selection is a good example of how Ovid interweaves
one metamorphosis-tale with another. The daughters of
Minyas sit around spinning, telling each other stories. So
before we hear of their fate, we get several 'tales within a
tale'. In 43ff., where Ovid describes the 'learned hesitation'
of the knowledgeable lady who eventually selects the story
of Pyramus and Thisbe out of all the other stories that occur
to her, he is of course showing off his own knowledge: in
the space of seven lines he gets in references to no less than
three other metamorphosis-tales; and in typical Hellenistic
fashion (see Introduction), the lady chooses the least well-
known one (l. 53).

Dionysus (with whom the Roman god Bacchus was
identified) was the Greek god of release and ecstasy—and
so, naturally, of wine. He is a foreign god, a latecomer to
Greece, and Homer (c. eighth century B.C.) has scarcely
heard of him. For this reason, quite apart from the fact
that he stands for the opposite of civilized living and does
not therefore find favour with the pillars of society, it is
likely that his worship was opposed by many cities as it
travelled west into Greece. This would explain the many
stories we find of opposition to his worship: by Lycurgos
of Thrace, who was punished by blindness; by Pentheus
King of Thebes, who was torn to pieces by his own mother;
and by the daughters of Proitos in Argos, who destroyed
their own children. The story of the opposition of the
daughters of Minyas is properly associated with the city
of Orchomenus rather than with Thebes.

As for Pyramus and Thisbe, it is worth noting that their story, so well known to us because of Shakespeare's *Midsummer Night's Dream*, where Bottom the weaver and his friends act it as a play in front of Theseus and his queen Hippolyta, was evidently not well known to Ovid's audience (*non vulgaris*, l. 53). The theme of the star-crossed young lovers, whose families oppose their relationship and who therefore have to elope and marry secretly, is one with which all mankind sympathizes, and it has been much used since: sometimes the story ends tragically, as in the double suicide which concludes Shakespeare's *Romeo and Juliet*; sometimes happily, as in the successful elopement of Porphyro and Madeleine in Keats' *Eve of St. Agnes*.

NOTES TO
'THE DAUGHTERS OF MINYAS'

1. *Alcithoe Minyeias:* two Greek forms: 'Alcithoe, daughter of Minyas'.
2. *accipienda:* sc. *esse.*
4. *celebrare:* this and subsequent infs. are dep. on *iusserat* (l. 8). Sc. *Ismenides* as subject of *celebrare* and first object of *iusserat.*
    sacerdos: subject of main verb *iusserat* (l 8).
5. *immunes* (agreeing with *famulas*) : sc. *esse* (dep. on *iusserat*).
    suorum: sc. *operum.* Tr. 'those who commanded their tasks', their mistresses.
6. *pectora:* acc. of extent. The subject of *tegi* is *dominas.*
    crinales solvere vittas: lit., to loosen their hair-ribbons.
7. *coma:* abl. 'in their hair'.
    thyrsos: a thyrsus was a wand wreathed with vine-leaves (*frondentis*), carried in honour of Bacchus.
8. *laesi:* conditional ptcpl. 'if he were slighted'.
10. *telas:* 'their looms' (as in l. 35 below).
    calathos: 'baskets' (of wool). These two words refer to the kind of tasks the women would have to lay aside in order to take part in the festival revels.
31. *Ismenides:* 'the women of Thebes', so called because the river Ismenus ran near Thebes.
    adsis: sc. *o Bacche.*
32. *Minyeides:* nom. plur.
33. *turbantes festa:* 'spoiling the festival'.
    intempestiva Minerva: abl. Minerva was the goddess of spinning and weaving (among other things), and the name is used here to refer to the process itself. Cp. Pallas in l. 38.

Book 4

4. THE DAUGHTERS OF MINYAS
(including the tale of
PYRAMUS AND THISBE)

The daughters of Minyas, alone out of all the women of Thebes, deny Bacchus and refuse to participate in his worship, choosing instead to stay at home and spin (1–35).

At non Alcithoe Minyeias orgia censet
accipienda dei, sed adhuc temeraria Bacchum
progeniem negat esse Iovis sociasque sorores
impietatis habet. Festum celebrare sacerdos
immunesque operum famulas dominasque suorum   5
pectora pelle tegi, crinales solvere vittas,
serta coma, manibus frondentis sumere thyrsos
iusserat, et saevam laesi fore numinis iram
vaticinatus erat; parent matresque nurusque
telasque calathosque infectaque pensa reponunt   10

(Here the tale is interrupted by an outburst of praise to Bacchus.)

'Placatus mitisque' rogant Ismenides 'adsis',
iussaque sacra colunt; solae Minyeides intus
intempestiva turbantes festa Minerva
aut ducunt lanas aut stamina pollice versant
aut haerent telae famulasque laboribus urgent.   35

(55)

36. *levi:* 'nimble', 'deft'.
38. *Pallas:* i.e., Pallas Athene, of whom Minerva is the Roman equivalent.
40. *per vices:* '(each) in turn'.
    aliquid: obj. of *referamus.*
41. *in medium:* 'for the general benefit (of us all)'.
42. *primam:* sc. *eam,* the one who suggested the idea.
43. *quid . . . referat:* indirect question dep. on *cogitat* in the next line.
    norat = noverat.
44 *narret:* deliberative subjunctive after *dubia est.* The alternative stories she might tell are each introduced by *an ut* ('or how') in the foll. lines.
44f. *Babylonia Derceti:* voc., 'Dercetis of Babylon', i.e., the Syrian goddess Atargatis.
45. *versa:* abl. agreeing with *figura* in the next line.
    squamis velantibus artus: i.e., she changed into a fish. The phrase is abl. absolute in the present tense, contemporaneous with the action described in the inf. *motasse.*
46. *Palaestini:* 'the Syrians'. Nom. subj. of *credunt.*
    motasse (motavisse): the subject is *quam* and the object *stagna.* Lit. 'to have moved', i.e., swum in.
47. *illius filia:* Semiramis, daughter of Dercetis, who was changed at death into a dove.
49. Take *an ut* first in translating: 'or how the nymph . . .'
52. *contactu:* casual abl.
53. *hoc:* 'this last idea'.
54. *orsa:* sc. *est.*
    lana . . . sequente: abl. absolute, lit. 'while the wool was following its threads'. The story-teller went on with her spinning while she told the tale.

One of the sisters suggests that they tell each other stories as they work; they agree, and she, after some deliberation, decides to start with the tale of Pyramus and Thisbe (36-54).

E quibus una levi deducens pollice filum
'Dum cessant aliae commentaque sacra frequentant,
nos quoque, quas Pallas, melior dea, detinet' inquit,
'utile opus manuum vario sermone levemus
perque vices aliquid, quod tempora longa videri   40
non sinat, in medium vacuas referamus ad aures!'
dicta probant primamque iubent narrare sorores.
Illa, quid e multis referat (nam plurima norat),
cogitat et dubia est, de te, Babylonia, narret,
Derceti, quam versa squamis velantibus artus   45
stagna Palaestini credunt motasse figura,
an magis, ut sumptis illius filia pennis
extremos albis in turribus egerit annos,
nais an ut cantu nimiumque potentibus herbis
verterit in tacitos iuvenalia corpora pisces,   50
donec idem passa est, an, quae poma alba ferebat
ut nunc nigra ferat contactu sanguinis arbor:
hoc placet, haec quoniam vulgaris fabula non est;
talibus orsa modis lana sua fila sequente:

Pyramus and Thisbe, the young lovers of Babylon, forbidden by their parents to marry or even associate, talk to each other through a chink in the wall of their adjacent houses; finally (84ff.) they agree to meet by night at the tree by Ninus' tomb, outside the city wall (55-92).

56. *quas:* the (postponed) antecedent is *puellis*.
58. *urbem:* Babylon, round which, legend says, the goddess Semiramis built a wall of bricks (*coctilibus*).
59. *notitiam primosque gradus:* hendiadys: 'the first stages *of* their acquaintance'.
60. *taedae . . . coissent:* lit. 'they would, too, have come together by the rightful process of the marriage torch', i.e., they'd have got married.
61. *quod* (acc.)*:* refers to the whole action described in the next line, i.e., their mutual love.
62. *ex aequo:* 'equally'.
    captis: sc. *amore.*
63. *conscius omnis abest:* i.e., they told nobody of their love.
64. *quoque magis . . . magis:* 'and the more . . . the more'.
    ignis (sc. *amoris*) is subj. of *tegitur* as well as of *aestuat.*
65. *fissus:* agreeing with *paries* in the next line.
66. *cum fieret:* 'when it was being built'.
67. *nulli:* dat. of the agent after *notatum*, 'noticed by no one'.
68. *vidistis:* the narrator addresses the lovers personally: 'you lovers first discovered it'.
74. *quantum erat:* lit. 'how much was it that you should . . .', i.e., 'was it *too* much to allow us . . . ?'
77. *quod:* 'the fact that', acts as obj. of *debere* in the previous line.
79. *sub noctem:* 'at nightfall'.
79f. *parti quisque suae:* 'each to their own side' is parenthetical, expanding on the main phrase *dedere oscula*; that is why the main verb is plural despite nom. sing. *quisque.*
80. *contra:* 'to the opposite side'.
81. *Aurora:* goddess of the dawn, used instead of the dawn itself, as often in Ovid.
84. *multa prius questi:* lit. 'after first uttering many complaints'.
84ff. *ut . . . temptent:* the *ut* clause, after *statuunt*, expresses what they decided to do. The subjunctives in the foll. lines (*relinquant, conveniant, lateant*) are still part of this *ut* clause.
87. *neve sit errandum:* lit. 'and so that they shouldn't have to wander'. *spatiantibus* is dat. of the agent after *errandum* (gerund of obligation).

'Pyramus et Thisbe, iuvenum pulcherrimus alter,   55
altera, quas Oriens habuit, praelata puellis,
contiguas tenuere domos, ubi dicitur altam
coctilibus muris cinxisse Semiramis urbem.
notitiam primosque gradus vicinia fecit,
tempore crevit amor; taedae quoque iure coissent   60
sed vetuere patres: quod non potuere vetare,
ex aequo captis ardebant mentibus ambo.
Conscius omnis abest; nutu signisque loquuntur,
quoque magis tegitur, tectus magis aestuat ignis.
Fissus erat tenui rima, quam duxerat olim,   65
cum fieret, paries domui communis utrique.
Id vitium nulli per saecula longa notatum—
quid non sentit amor?—primi vidistis amantes
et vocis fecistis iter, tutaeque per illud
murmure blanditiae minimo transire solebant.   70
Saepe, ubi constiterant hinc Thisbe, Pyramus illinc,
inque vices fuerat captatus anhelitus oris,
'Invide' dicebant 'paries, quid amantibus obstas?
quantum erat, ut sineres toto nos corpore iungi
aut, hoc si nimium est, vel ad oscula danda pateres?   75
nec sumus ingrati; tibi nos debere fatemur,
quod datus est verbis ad amicas transitus auris.'
talia diversa nequiquam sede locuti
sub noctem dixere 'Vale' partique dedere
oscula quisque suae non pervenientia contra.   80
Postera nocturnos Aurora removerat ignes,
solque pruinosas radiis siccaverat herbas:
ad solitum coiere locum. Tum murmure parvo
multa prius questi statuunt, ut nocte silenti
fallere custodes foribusque excedere temptent,   85
cumque domo exierint, urbis quoque tecta relinquant,
neve sit errandum lato spatiantibus arvo,

88. *busta Nini:* Shakespeare's 'Ninny's tomb'. *Ninus* was King of Assyria and husband of Semiramis.
91. *pacta:* lit., 'the things they'd agreed on'.
 visa: lit. 'having seemed'. Tr. 'which had seemed'.
92. *praecipitatur aquis:* 'sinks into the waters (of ocean)'.

94. *suos:* sc. *parentes.*
 vultum: acc. of space over which.
95. *dicta* = *pacta.*
96. *audacem:* sc. *eam.*
97. *spumantis oblita rictus:* retained acc. after a passive verb. The active form of the expression would be *oblino rictus caede,* 'I smear her jaws with blood'; here the acc. *rictus* is retained even though the verb is passive (*oblita*).
98. *depositura:* lit. 'going to quench', i.e., 'in order to quench'.
99. *quam:* the antecedent is *leaena* in the prec. sentence.
 ad: here 'by'.
 Babylonia: ornate, learned epithet: 'of Babylon'.
101. *tergo:* abl. of separation with *lapsa,* 'from her shoulders'.
103. *inventos:* agreeing with *amictus* in the next line.
 sine ipsa: 'without (the girl) herself (in it)'.
104. *amictus:* plur. for sing., as *velamina* in l. 101.
105. *egressus:* sc. *Pyramus* (l. 107).
110. *nostra* = *mea* (cp. l. 112), 'my soul', i.e., I myself.

conveniant ad busta Nini lateantque sub umbra
arboris: arbor ibi niveis uberrima pomis
(ardua morus erat) gelido contermina fonti.   90
Pacta placent; et lux, tarde discedere visa,
praecipitatur aquis, et aquis nox exit ab isdem.

Thisbe, arriving first at the rendezvous, meets a
lioness and escapes into a cave, but drops her veil
behind her (93–101); the lioness, her jaws still
bloody from hunting, tears at the veil; Pyramus,
arriving and finding the bloodstained veil, concludes that Thisbe must be dead, and kills himself
(119), his blood staining the berries of the tree
(102–27).

Callida per tenebras versato cardine Thisbe
egreditur fallitque suos adopertaque vultum
pervenit ad tumulum dictaque sub arbore sedit.   95
Audacem faciebat amor. Venit ecce recenti
caede leaena boum spumantis oblita rictus
depositura sitim vicini fontis in unda;
quam procul ad lunae radios Babylonia Thisbe
vidit et obscurum timido pede fugit in antrum,   100
dumque fugit, tergo velamina lapsa reliquit.
Ut lea saeva sitim multa compescuit unda,
dum redit in silvas, inventos forte sine ipsa
ore cruentato tenues laniavit amictus.
Serius egressus vestigia vidit in alto   105
pulvere certa ferae totoque expalluit ore
Pyramus; ut vero vestem quoque sanguine tinctam
repperit, 'Una duos' inquit 'nox perdet amantes,
e quibus illa fuit longa dignissima vita;
nostra nocens anima est. Ego te, miseranda, peremi,   110

111. *qui:* take first in translating.

112. *divellite:* imperative (subj. *leones,* l. 114).

115. *timidi:* 'characterizing' genitive: 'it is the coward's part . . .'
   optare necem: i.e., at the hands of another, rather than bravely killing oneself.
   Thisbes: Greek gen. 'Thisbe's'.

117. Rhetorical repetition of *dedit.* Take *notae* with *vesti* and tr. them last.

118. *accipe haustus.* 'take draughts of', i.e., drink. He is addressing Thisbe's veil, stained (he thinks) with her own blood already.

119. *quo:* the antecedent is *ferrum.*

120. *nec mora:* sc. *erat.* 'And without delay . . .'

121. *emicat alte:* 'shoots out in a high jet'.

122. *cum:* conjunction not preposition. *vitiato plumbo* is descriptive abl. with *fistula.*

123. *tenui stridente foramine:* abl. absolute.

124. *ictibus:* 'with the force of its impact', lit. 'with impacts'.

128. *amantem:* 'her lover', Pyramus.

129. *illa:* Thisbe.
   oculis animoque: hendiadys. Tr. 'eagerly looks around for'.

130. *narrare* is inf. after *gestit* and governs the indirect question *quanta pericula vita(ve)rit.*

131f. *utque . . . sic:* 'and although . . . yet'.

131. *visa in arbore formam:* an odd way of saying 'the shape *of* the tree (she had) seen (before)'.

132. *haeret, an haec sit:* a highly compressed phrase; of which the full version would be something like *haeret mente, an haec sit arbor quam prius vidisset.*

133f. *tremebunda . . . solum:* a gruesome description of the death-throes of Pyramus. *tremebunda* is acc. plur. agreeing with *membra.*

(62)

in loca plena metus qui iussi nocte venires
nec prior huc veni. Nostrum divellite corpus
et scelerata fero consumite viscera morsu,
O quicumque sub hac habitatis rupe leones!
Sed timidi est optare necem'. Velamina Thisbes   115
tollit et ad pactae secum fert arboris umbram,
utque dedit notae lacrimas, dedit oscula vesti,
'Accipe nunc' inquit, 'nostri quoque sanguinis haustus!'
quoque erat accinctus, demisit in ilia ferrum,
nec mora, ferventi moriens e vulnere traxit.   120
Ut iacuit resupinus humo, cruor emicat alte,
non aliter quam cum vitiato fistula plumbo
scinditur et tenui stridente foramine longas
eiaculatur aquas atque ictibus aera rumpit.
Arborei fetus aspergine caedis in atram   125
vertuntur faciem, madefactaque sanguine radix
purpureo tinguit pendentia mora colore.

> Thisbe, returning, finds Pyramus dead, and kills
> herself, after making two prayers, both of which
> were granted; that they should be buried together,
> and that the tree's fruit should be forever blood-red
> in remembrance of their deaths (128–66).

Ecce metu nondum posito, ne fallat amantem,
illa redit iuvenemque oculis animoque requirit,
quantaque vitarit narrare pericula gestit;   130
utque locum et visa cognoscit in arbore formam,
sic facit incertam pomi color: haeret, an haec sit.
Dum dubitat, tremebunda videt pulsare cruentum
membra solum, retroque pedem tulit, oraque buxo
pallidiora gerens exhorruit aequoris instar,   135
quod tremit, exigua cum summum stringitur aura.

137. *remorata:* 'checking herself' in her withdrawal (l. 134).
    amores: abstract for concrete. The meaning is exactly
    the same as that of *amantem* in l. 128.
139. *laniata comas: comas* is direct obj. of the verb. This use
    of the passive as if the verb were deponent like *amplector,*
    is in imitation of the Greek *middle* voice.
141. *vultibus:* plur. for sing.
142. *mihi:* ethic dat. instead of abl. of separation.
146. *visa illa* (sc. *Thisbe*): abl. absolute. Supply *oculos* as
    obj. of *recondidit.*
147. *ense:* abl. after *vacuum* in the next line.
149. *in unum hoc:* 'for this one (deed)'; because, being
    suicide, it will be her last.
150. *hic:* sc. *amor meus.*
    vulnera: plur. for sing.
151. *extinctum:* sc. *te,* as obj. of *persequar.*
152. *morte:* instrumental abl. in this and the next line.
153. *revelli:* supply *a me* over again from the relative clause.
154. lit. 'but be asked this by the words of both (me and
    P.)', i.e., we ask this favour of you. *Hoc* refers to the *ut*
    clause in lines 156–7.
155. *meus illiusque:* is in apposition to the rest of the line:
    'my (father) and his (P.'s)'.
156. *hora novissima:* 'the newest hour', i.e., the last hour, the
    hour of death.
157. *componi eodem tumulo* (with *eos* understood as antecedent
    to *quos* in the prec. line), is acc. and inf. after *invideatis.*
158. *arbor* (voc.): in retarded position; tr. after *tu.*
159. *duorum:* sc. *miserabilia corpora.*
162. *pectus sub imum:* lit. 'under her lowest breast', pleonas-
    tic for 'beneath her breast'. She was poised over the
    sword-point, ready to fall on it.
164. *tetigere:* 'touched', i.e., were successful with. For the
    gods granted the prayer she'd made in l. 58–61, and her
    parents the prayer in l. 54–7.
166. *quodque rogis superest:* this relative clause is subj. of
    requiescit.

Sed postquam remorata suos cognovit amores,
percutit indignos claro plangore lacertos
et laniata comas amplexaque corpus amatum
vulnera supplevit lacrimis fletumque cruori   140
miscuit et gelidis in vultibus oscula figens
'Pyrame', clamavit, 'quis te mihi casus ademit?
Pyrame, responde! Tua te carissima Thisbe
nominat; exaudi vultusque attolle iacentes!'
Ad nomen Thisbes oculos a morte gravatos   145
Pyramus erexit visaque recondidit illa.
Quae postquam vestemque suam cognovit et ense
vidit ebur vacuum, 'Tua te manus' inquit, 'amorque
perdidit, infelix! Est et mihi fortis in unum
hoc manus, est et amor: dabit hic in vulnera vires.   150
Persequar extinctum letique miserrima dicar
causa comesque tui: quique a me morte revelli
heu sola poteras, poteris nec morte revelli.
Hoc tamen amborum verbis estote rogati,
O multum miseri meus illiusque parentes,   155
ut, quos certus amor, quos hora novissima iunxit,
componi tumulo non invideatis eodem;
at tu quae ramis arbor miserabile corpus
nunc tegis unius, mox es tectura duorum,
signa tene caedis pullosque et luctibus aptos   160
semper habe fetus, gemini monimenta cruoris.'
Dixit, et aptato pectus mucrone sub imum
incubuit ferro, quod adhuc a caede tepebat.
Vota tamen tetigere deos, tetigere parentes;
nam color in pomo est, ubi permaturuit, ater,   165
quodque rogis superest, una requiescit in urna.'

The other daughters of Minyas tell tales (167–
388, omitted). Then the vengeance of Bacchus de-

392. *adunco cornu:* descriptive abl., 'with curved end'.

393. *redolent:* best tr. 'there is a scent of . . .'

394. *resque fide maior:* nom. in apposition to the rest of the sentence, lit. 'a thing greater than credibility', past belief.

395. *pendens:* sc. from the loom.

396. *abit:* i.e., disappears, 'changes'.

396f. *et . . . exit:* Ovid does not provide a technically exact account, but an impressionistic picture of the threads of the loom (*fila*) turning into vine-tendrils (*palmes*), and of vine-foliage, leaves and all (*pampinus*) bursting out from the vertical, harder-twisted threads which formed the warp (*stamen*).

398. i.e., the purple colour of the woven cloth is transferred to the purple colour of the grapes.

400. *quod:* the antecedent is *tempus*. In translating the line, postpone the second *nec* till just before *lucem*.

401. A difficult line. Lit. 'but (you could call the time) the border-territory (*confinia* plur. for sing.) of uncertain night, with light nevertheless'.

406. *diversae locis:* Lit. 'various in their locations'. Tr. 'in various places'.

407. *dumque petunt tenebras:* note the appropriateness of the moment for a bat-metamorphosis.

   parvos: 'slender'.

409. *qua . . . figuram:* indirect question introduced by *scire* in the next line. Tr. *qua ratione* together: 'in what way'.

410. *non pluma:* because a bat's wing is 'leathern'.

412. *et pro corpore:* 'and in keeping with their (tiny) body'.

415. *nomen:* i.e., *vespertilio,* a bat.

(66)

scends; their looms turn into vines (394–8), their house seems to catch fire (399–406), and they themselves are changed into bats (407–15).

Finis erat dictis, sed adhuc Minyeia proles
urget opus spernitque deum festumque profanat,   390
tympana cum subito non apparentia raucis
obstrepuere sonis, et adunco tibia cornu
tinnulaque aera sonant; redolent murraeque crocique
resque fide maior, coepere virescere telae
inque hederae faciem pendens frondescere vestis;   395
pars abit in vites, et quae modo fila fuerunt,
palmite mutantur; de stamine pampinus exit;
purpura fulgorem pictis accomodat uvis.
Iamque dies exactus erat, tempusque subibat,
quod tu nec tenebras nec possis dicere lucem,   400
sed cum luce tamen dubiae confinia noctis;
tecta repente quati pinguesque ardere videntur
lampades et rutilis collucere ignibus aedes
falsaque saevarum simulacra ululare ferarum,
fumida iamdudum latitant per tecta sorores   405
diversaeque locis ignes ac lumina vitant,
dumque petunt tenebras, parvos membrana per artus
porrigitur tenuique includit bracchia pinna;
nec qua perdiderint veterem ratione figuram,
scire sinunt tenebrae; non illas pluma levavit,   410
sustinuere tamen se perlucentibus alis
conataeque loqui minimam et pro corpore vocem
emittunt peraguntque levi stridore querellas.
Tectaque, non silvas, celebrant lucemque perosae
nocte volant seroque tenent a vespere nomen.   415

5

Proserpina

INTRODUCTION TO 'PROSERPINA'

The name Proserpina is a corruption of the Greek name
Persephone. The goddess Persephone is identified in Greek
literature with Kore, the Greek corn-maiden, daughter of
Demeter. Similarly Hades, the god of the underworld, is
identified with Pluto (whose name means 'Wealth'), god of
fertility. It is not certain what Persephone's original function was, but it is tempting to suppose that she was originally
a goddess of death, and that the connexion in men's minds
of death with fertility was the reason why she became
identified with Kore, and Hades with Pluto.

The connexion of death with fertility is in the first place
an agricultural one. Planting a seed in the ground is in
effect giving burial to a relic of last year's crop. The Somer-
set folk-song 'John Barleycorn' is about this miracle of the
seed: you may use John Barleycorn 'right barbarouslee',
cut him 'off at knee' with your scythes, whip him with
flails, and then bury him—but you cannot kill him; on the
contrary, 'Except a corn of wheat fall into the ground and
die, it abideth alone: but if it die, it bringeth forth much
fruit' (John xii. 24). If we think of the dependence of man
on the success of the harvest, we understand both the im-
portance and the antiquity of the story of Persephone.

The oldest literary account of it is in the Homeric Hymn
to Demeter, of the seventh century B.C. But cuneiform texts
as old as 1000 B.C. tell how Mesopotamian goddesses of fertility were kept in the underworld and then returned to
earth.

In Ovid, as we should expect, the solemn and reverent tone in which the Homeric Hymn told this story has altogether disappeared. Proserpina, like any ordinary little girl, has time to be worried about losing her flowers in the middle of being abducted (400f.); Jupiter himself displays a very human vanity (525f.). Ovid shows much ingenuity in working other metamorphoses into the main tale: summaries of these are given in the text.

NOTES TO 'PROSERPINA'

385. *Hennaeis moenibus:* 'the city of Henna', a very old seat of the worship of the corn-goddess.
386. *illo:* sc. *lacu.* comparative abl.
    Caystros: nom. a river in Lydia famous for its swans.
389. *ut velo:* 'as with an awning'.
390. *tyrios:* this adjective may be used to mean any bright colour, usually purple, from the famous purple dye of Tyre.
391ff. The Homeric hymn (see Introd.) says that Hades caused a beautiful flower to grow, and that when Persephone plucked it, the earth opened and Hades appeared with his chariot.
394. *aequales:* 'her companions', lit. 'age-fellows'.
395. *Diti:* dat. of the agent, from *Dis.*
396. *usque adeo:* lit. 'right up to such an extent'. *usque* is simply strengthening *adeo.*
    maesto: agreeing with *ore* in the next line.
398. *summa ab ora:* 'from the upper edge (of the dress)'.
    laniarat = laniaverat.

402. *quemque:* sc. *equum*, 'each horse'.
403. *per:* 'along'.
404. *ferrugine:* lit. the colour of iron, and so any very dark colour; even the harness of the horses of the god of the underworld was black.

Book 5

5. PROSERPINA

Proserpina is abducted by Dis (Pluto) while gathering flowers in a wood near Henna in Sicily (385-404).

Haud procul Hennaeis lacus est a moenibus altae,   385
nomine Pergus, aquae: non illo plura Caystros
carmina cycnorum labentibus audit in undis.
Silva coronat aquas cingens latus omne, suisque
frondibus ut velo Phoebeos submovet ictus;
frigora dant rami, tyrios humus umida flores: 390
perpetuum ver est. Quo dum Proserpina luco
ludit et aut violas aut candida lilia carpit,
dumque puellari studio calathosque sinumque
implet et aequales certat superare legendo,
paene simul visa est dilectaque raptaque Diti;   395
usque adeo est properatus amor. Dea territa maesto
et matrem et comites, sed matrem saepius, ore
clamat, et ut summa vestem laniarat ab ora,
collecti flores tunicis cecidere remissis,
tantaque simplicitas puerilibus adfuit annis,   400
haec quoque virgineum movit iactura dolorem.
Raptor agit currus et nomine quemque vocando
exhortatur equos, quorum per colla iubasque
excutit obscura tinctas ferrugine habenas. . . .

438. *matri:* dat. of the agent after pf. pass. *quaesita est.*

440. *udis capillis:* because of morning dew.
441. *Hesperus:* the evening star.
442. *Aetna:* Etna, the Sicilian volcano.
444. *hebeta (ve) rat:* lit. 'had made dull', i.e., dimmed.
445. i.e., from West to East.

462. forms an indirect question introduced by *dicere longa mora est* at the beginning of the next line. Lit. 'it is a long delay to say through what lands . . .'
463. *quaerenti defuit orbis:* lit. 'the world was lacking to her as she sought', i.e., she had sought everywhere on earth.
464. *Sicaniam:* Sicily (acc.).
466. *volenti:* sc. *ei*, the nymph Cyane.
467. *nec . . . habebat:* understand *quicquam* as obj. of *habebat* and antecedent of *quo* (which is instrumental abl.).
468. *notam:* agreeing with *zonam* in l. 470.
    parenti: sc. of Persephone.

Lines 405–37 (omitted) tell of the metamorphosis of Cyane, nymph of the fountain of that name, who incurred the anger of Pluto by warning him of the consequences of what he had done; she was changed into water, thus becoming a part of her own fountain.
Ceres searches for her daughter day and night (438–45).

Interea pavidae nequiquam filia matri
omnibus est terris, omni quaesita profundo.
Illam non udis veniens Aurora capillis   440
cessantem vidit, non Hesperus; illa duabus
flammiferas pinus manibus succendit ab Aetna
perque pruinosas tulit irrequieta tenebras;
rursus ubi alma dies hebetarat sidera, natam
solis ab occasu solis quaerebat ad ortus. . . .   445

In lines 446–61 (omitted), Ovid works in another metamorphosis; Ceres, while drinking a beverage prepared for her by a kind old lady, is mocked by the old lady's grandson, and punishes him by changing him into a lizard.
Ceres finds her daughter's girdle, and puts a blight upon the earth (462–86).

Quas dea per terras et quas erraverit undas,
dicere longa mora est; quaerenti defuit orbis;
Sicaniam repetit, dumque omnia lustrat eundo,
venit et ad Cyanen. Ea ni mutata fuisset,   465
omnia narrasset; sed et os et lingua volenti
dicere non aderant, nec, quo loqueretur, habebat;
signa tamen manifesta dedit notamque parenti,

470. *Persephones:* Greek gen.

471. *raptam(esse):* sc. *filiam.*

472. *scisset = scivisset.*

473. *repetita:* agrees with *pectora.* Tr. 'again and again'.

474. *sit:* the subject is *Persephone.*

476. *Trinacriam:* sc. *increpat,* another name for Sicily.

    vestigia damni: 'signs of her loss', i.e., Persephone's girdle.

477. be careful to *scan* this line in order to find out what *saeva* agrees with.

478. *parili:* adj. agreeing with *leto.* Tr. adverbially, 'alike'.

480. *fallere depositum:* lit. 'to deceive their trust', i.e., to spoil the seed entrusted to them.

482. *falsa iacet:* lit. 'lies low, discredited'. The subject is technically *fertilitas,* but in sense *fama fertilitatis,* the land's *reputation* for fertility.

    primis in herbis: lit. '(while still) in the earliest blade', i.e., soon after appearing above the ground.

484. *sidera:* 'stormy seasons'.

485. *iacta legunt:* 'peck up (the seeds) as soon as they are sown'.

486. *gramen:* this is nom., joint subject with *lolium tribulique.*

487. *Alpheias:* the nymph and fountain Arethusa, whose waters were supposed to unite with those of the river Alpheus, which flows through Elis in the Peloponnese (hence *Eleis* (adj. 'of Elis') *undis*).

489. *toto orbe:* with *quaesitae,* lit. 'sought over the whole world'.

491. *neve irascere:* 'and don't be angry'. *violenta* is nom.

492. *patuit rapinae:* lit. 'opened to the robbery'. According to Ovid, Pluto had hurled his sceptre at the earth and caused it to open for his chariot when he was abducting Proserpina (ll. 420–4, omitted).

494. *Pisa:* a city of *Elis* (gen. *Elidis*), on the river Alpheus, near which the Olympic games were held.

    ab Elide ducimus ortus: lit. 'I take my origin from Elis' (*ducimus,* plur. for sing.).

495. *omni:* agreeing with *solo* in the next line, which is a comparative abl.

497. *quam:* the antecedent is *sedem.*

illo forte loco delapsam in gurgite sacro
Persephones zonam summis ostendit in undis.   470
Quam simul agnovit, tamquam tum denique raptam
scisset, inornatos laniavit diva capillos
et repetita suis percussit pectora palmis.
nescit adhuc, ubi sit; terras tamen increpat omnes
ingratasque vocat nec frugum munere dignas,   475
Trinacriam ante alias, in qua vestigia damni
repperit. Ergo illic saeva vertentia glaebas
fregit aratra manu parilique irata colonos
ruricolasque boves leto dedit arvaque iussit
fallere depositum vitiataque semina fecit.   480
Fertilitas terrae latum vulgata per orbem
falsa iacet; primis segetes moriuntur in herbis,
et modo sol nimius, nimius modo corripit imber;
sideraque ventique nocent, avidaeque volucres
semina iacta legunt; lolium tribulique fatigant   485
triticeas messes et inexpugnabile gramen.

The nymph Arethusa tells Ceres that Proserpina
is now the wife of Pluto (487–508).

Tum caput Eleis Alpheias extulit undis
rorantesque comas a fronte removit ad aures
atque ait 'O toto quaesitae virginis orbe
et frugum genetrix, immensos siste labores   490
neve tibi fidae violenta irascere terrae.
Terra nihil meruit, patuitque invita rapinae,
nec sum pro patria supplex: huc hospita veni.
Pisa mihi patria est et ab Elide ducimus ortus,
Sicaniam peregrina colo, sed gratior omni   495
haec mihi terra solo est: hos nunc Arethusa penates,
hanc habeo sedem. Quam tu, mitissima, serva.

498–500. *mota . . . Ortygiam* forms an indirect question introduced by *hora veniet narratibus:* 'there will come a time (lit. hour) suitable to tell you (lit. for my narrations as to . . .) why I have been moved from my place', etc.

500. *levata:* nom. agreeing with *tu* (Ceres). Tr. 'when you will both (*-que*) be relieved of your worry and (will be) of a better countenance'. This comes true, l. 570.

501. *vultus melioris:* i.e., you will be smiling instead of looking sad.

502. *subterque . . . cavernas:* 'flowing away beneath deep-down caverns'.

504. *labor:* pres. indicative, as usual in this type of *dum-*clause.

  Stygio . . . gurgite: 'in my Stygian stream'. *Stygius,* the adj. from *Styx* (the river in the underworld) is here used to convey the depth below the earth to which Arethusa's stream descends.

506. *tristis:* sc. *est,* as again with *regina* in the next line.

507. *opaci mundi:* lit. 'of the dark world', the underworld.

509. *ad auditas voces:* lit. 'at the heard voices', and so 'on hearing what she said'.

510. *ut . . . amentia:* lit. 'and when her great madness was driven away by her great grief'.

511f. *oras . . . aetherias:* 'she goes up (lit. out) into the regions of heaven'.

513. *ante Iovem:* according to the Homeric Hymn version, there had been collusion between Jupiter (Zeus) and Pluto (Hades) before the abduction, but Ovid ignores this part of the tale.

515. *si . . . matris:* 'if her mother has no influence', i.e., if *I* cannot move you.

516f. *neu . . . partu:* lit. 'and let there not to you be less care, I pray, of the fact (*illius*) that she was brought forth by *my* parturition', i.e., have equal regard for the fact that she is *your* daughter, and that *I'm* her mother. The same double point is made in 522.

Mota loco cur sim tantique per aequoris undas
advehar Ortygiam, veniet narratibus hora
tempestiva meis, cum tu curaque levata   500
et vultus melioris eris. Mihi pervia tellus
praebet iter, subterque imas ablata cavernas
hic caput attollo desuetaque sidera cerno.
Ergo dum Stygio sub terris gurgite labor,
visa tua est oculis illic Proserpina nostris: 505
illa quidem tristis neque adhuc interrita vultu,
sed regina tamen, sed opaci maxima mundi,
sed tamen inferni pollens matrona tyranni!'

Ceres complains to Jupiter, Proserpina's father
(509–22); he says Pluto is not an unworthy son-in-
law, but agrees that Proserpina shall rejoin her
mother, provided that she has not eaten any food
in the Underworld (523–32); unfortunately, Proserpina had eaten seven pomegranate seeds (533–
8).

Mater ad auditas stupuit ceu saxea voces
attonitaeque diu similis fuit, utque dolore   510
pulsa gravi gravis est amentia, curribus oras
exit in aetherias: ibi toto nubila vultu
ante Iovem passis stetit invidiosa capillis
'Pro' que 'meo veni supplex tibi, Iuppiter,' inquit
'sanguine proque tuo; si nulla est gratia matris,   515
nata patrem moveat, neu sit tibi cura, precamur,
vilior illius, quod nostro est edita partu.
En quaesita diu tandem mihi nata reperta est,
si reperire vocas amittere certius, aut si
Scire, ubi sit, reperire vocas. Quod rapta, feremus,   520
dummodo reddat eam! Neque enim praedone marito

519f. *si . . . vocas:* lit. 'if you call more certain loss (*amittere certius*) "finding", or if you call knowing where she is (*scire ubi sit*) "finding her" '.

521f. *quod . . . eam:* lit. 'we (I) will bear the fact that she has been abducted (*rapta*, sc. *est*), provided that he gives her back'.

523. *excepit:* 'answered'.

524. *nomina . . . vera:* i.e., call things by their true names.

525. *non . . . est:* 'this deed is not an injury, but (a sign of) love'.

526. *pudori:* predicative dat., 'a source of shame'.

527. *modo = dummodo*, 'provided that you are willing'.
    ut desint cetera: i.e., to say nothing of his other qualities. Lit. 'that his other qualities may be lacking'.

528. *quid, quod:* lit. 'what of the fact that . . . ?' Tr. simply, 'But in fact . . .'

529. i.e., he is my equal in everything except fortune.

530. *discidii:* between Pluto and Proserpina.

531. *lege tamen certa:* 'but on one unalterable condition'. The condition is stated in the following six words.

532. *nam . . . cautum est:* lit. 'for this proviso has been made by agreement of the Fates' i.e., it is unalterable destiny. The *Parcae* were the three goddesses of Fate: their names were Clotho, Lachesis, and Atropos.

533. *certum est:* lit. 'it is certain (resolve) for Ceres (*Cereri*, dat.) to . . .', she is resolved to get her daughter back.

534f. *ieiunia solverat:* 'had broken her fast'.

536. *poeniceum pomum:* lit. 'a Carthaginian apple', i.e., a pomegranate.

537. *septem:* acc. to the Homeric Hymn, it was just *one* seed, and she had to spend one *third* of each year with Hades.

538. *presserat:* 'had swallowed'.

564. *medius:* with gen., 'acting as mediator between'.

565. *ex aequo:* 'equally'.

filia digna tua est, si iam mea filia non est.'
Iuppiter excepit 'Commune est pignus onusque
nata mihi tecum; sed si modo nomina rebus
addere vera placet, non hoc iniuria factum,   525
verum amor est; neque erit nobis gener ille pudori,
tu modo, diva, velis. Ut desint cetera, quantum est
esse Iovis fratrem! Quid, quod nec cetera desunt
nec cedit nisi sorte mihi?—sed tanta cupido
si tibi discidii est, repetet Proserpina caelum,   530
lege tamen certa, si nullos contigit illic
ore cibos; nam sic Parcarum foedere cautum est.'
  Dixerat, at Cereri certum est educere natam;
non ita fata sinunt, quoniam ieiunia virgo
solverat et, cultis dum simplex errat in hortis,   535
poeniceum curva decerpserat arbore pomum
sumptaque pallenti septem de cortice grana
presserat ore suo. . . .

> Lines 539–563 (omitted) tell of the metamorphosis
> of Ascalaphus, who was the only witness of Proser-
> pina eating the pomegranate seeds, and informed
> against her, and was therefore changed by her into
> an owl (the bird of ill-omen); and of the daughters
> of Achelous, who had been gathering flowers with
> Proserpina when she was abducted, and were
> changed into Sirens (birds with the faces of
> women).
> Jupiter arranges for Proserpina to live half the
> year with her mother and half with her husband.
> Ceres' joy (564–71).

  At medius fratrisque sui maestaeque sororis
Iuppiter ex aequo volventem dividit annum;   565

566. *dea:* Proserpina, as in line 396.

   regnorum . . . duorum: 'a divinity common to (shared by) both kingdoms'.

567. sc. *menses* with the first *totidem:* 'She spends the same number of months with her mother as with her husband'.

568. *vertitur:* from grief to joy.

   facies: sc. *Cereris* (gen.). Here means 'state', 'condition'.

569. *Diti:* dat. of *Dis* (Pluto). The fact that Ceres looked gloomy even to 'gloomy Dis' shows just how sad she'd been.

570f. *ut sol,* etc.: Perhaps the literary origin of Shakespeare's:
   'Even so my sun one early morn did shine,
      With all triumphant splendour on my brow;
   But out alack, he was but one hour mine,
      The *region cloud hath masked him* from me now.'

nunc dea, regnorum numen commune duorum,
cum matre est totidem, totidem cum coniuge menses.
Vertitur extemplo facies et mentis et oris;
nam modo quae poterat Diti quoque maesta videri,
laeta deae frons est, ut sol, qui tectus aquosis   570
nubibus ante fuit, victis e nubibus exit.

6

Philemon and Baucis

INTRODUCTION TO 'PHILEMON
AND BAUCIS'

This story culminates in another tree-metamorphosis (cp.
No. 2, 'Apollo and Daphne', and the end of No. 3, 'Phaethon'). It is also another tale within a tale. King Theseus
was held up on a journey by the swollen waters of the river
Achelous. The river-god bade Theseus enter his house and
wait till the floods subsided. Since there were other guests
there too, there was a perfect setting for a series of stories
(cp. No. 4, 'The Daughters of Minyas'). First Achelous told
a story of how some islands they could see had come into
being, and then one of the guests, Lelex, told this story
about an oak and a linden tree in Phrygia, as an instance
of the power of the gods to change the landscape, or to
change people.

The story is a Phrygian version of the flood. It is ob-
viously like the story of Noah, and like another story which
Ovid had told in the first book of the *Metamorphoses*, of
how Deucalion and his wife Pyrrha were saved from the
flood because of their reverence.

It is a moral fable. Just as the story of Phaethon implies
a 'Don't', so this one imples a 'Do'. It is a simple tale of
Virtue Rewarded (and Vice Punished). Ovid's telling stres-
ses the moral: Philemon and Baucis are shown as content
with little (633f.), a perfect partnership (635f.), full of
goodwill (which is the chief adornment of their feast, 677f.).
They are models of 'natural piety': when they are told, like
Phaethon and Midas, that they can have anything they
like, what they choose is in striking contrast to what the

other two chose (707ff.). Above all, they have humility: when they see the miracle of the wine (682ff.), instead of realising that they are highly favoured, they imagine that they must have offended the gods by their shortcomings, and hastily prepare to sacrifice their solitary goose.

Ovid is in fact 'selling' the country life. In his account of the preparations for the meal, and of the meal itself, he is sniping by implication at the luxury of his contemporaries (Augustus tried, without success, to enforce measures against extravagance). To do this was the fashion among the Augustan poets: Virgil wrote his *Georgics* out of his own first-hand experience of farming in order to win esteem for the country way of life; and Tibullus (48–19 B.C.) in his elegies, and Horace in his Satires and Epistles, express a preference for rustic simplicity and peace.

NOTES TO
'PHILEMON AND BAUCIS'

624. *hinc:* 'from here', i.e., from the place Lelex has referred to in the prec. lines—an oak next to a linden-tree, surrounded by a low wall.

627. *Atlantiades:* 'the descendant of Atlas'. Mercury, son of Jupiter and grandson of Atlas.

    caducifer: 'carrying the *caduceus*, the wand with two serpents twined round it; this and the winged sandals (*alae*) were Mercury's insignia.

628. *locum requiemque:* hendiadys, 'a place to rest'.

632. *illa . . . illa:* abl. in anaphora, both agreeing with *casa* in the next line.

    iuncti: 'joined' (in marriage).

633f. *paupertatemque . . . ferendo.* 'and by freely admitting their poverty and bearing it without discontent (*nec iniqua mente* = lit. 'and not with hostile mind'), they made it light'.

635. *nec refert:* 'and it makes no difference'; followed by subjunctive without *utrum:* '. . . whether you ask for masters or (*-ne* for *an*) servants in that house (*illic*).

636. *idem:* nom. plur.

637. *penates:* the word has degenerated into meaning no more than *domum* here.

638. *summisso vertice:* 'with bended head' to get through the *humiles postes.*

639. *iussit:* 'he bade'. sc. *caelicolas* as obj.

640. *textum rude:* 'a rough-woven rug'.

644f. *tecto detulit:* 'brought down from the roof', i.e., from the roof-room, the garret.

Book 8

6. PHILEMON AND BAUCIS

Lelex tells a story of how Jupiter and Mercury came to the district, seeking hospitality, and were offered it only by an old couple of humble means, Philemon and Baucis (624–50).

Haud procul hinc stagnum est, tellus habitabilis olim,
nunc celebres mergis fulicisque palustribus undae;   625
Iuppiter huc specie mortali cumque parente
venit Atlantiades positis caducifer alis.
Mille domos adiere locum requiemque petentes,
mille domos clausere serae; tamen una recepit,
parva quidem, stipulis et canna tecta palustri,   630
sed pia Baucis anus parilique aetate Philemon
illa sunt annis iuncti iuvenalibus, illa
consenuere casa paupertatemque fatendo
effecere levem nec iniqua mente ferendo;
nec refert, dominos illic famulosne requiras: 635
tota domus duo sunt, idem parentque iubentque.
Ergo ubi caelicolae parvos tetigere penates
summissoque humiles intrarunt vertice postes,
membra senex posito iussit relevare sedili;
quo superiniecit textum rude sedula Baucis   640
inque foco tepidum cinerem dimovit et ignes
suscitat hesternos foliisque et cortice sicco
nutrit et ad flammas anima producit anili
multifidasque faces ramaliaque arida tecto

645. *admovit:* i.e., put them under the cooking pot.

646. *quodque:* the antecedent to *quod* is *holus* in the next line.

647. *truncat holus foliis:* 'she strips the cabbage of its leaves'.

648. *terga:* 'the chine-piece', hung from the rafters in order to get smoked.

    suis: gen. of *sus*.

650. *domat:* here 'boils'.

660. *tremens:* not from age, but out of natural nervousness.

662f. *clivum sustulit:* lit. 'removed the slope', made the table level.

664. *bicolor . . . Minervae:* i.e., the olive. *bicolor* because the olive may be either green or black. The olive was the gift of Athena to Athens (Minerva is the Roman counterpart to Athena). *sincerae:* 'uncorrupted'.

665. *Scan* this line before translating.

666. Three examples of simple fare. *Lac coactum* ('curdled milk', i.e., cream cheese) was part of the staple diet of the shepherd Cyclops, the giant in Homer's Odyssey.

667. *leviter versata:* lit. 'lightly turned', i.e., lightly cooked (cp. the phrase 'done to a turn').

668. *omnia fictilibus:* sc. *ponuntur* from l. 664.

668f. *caelatus eodem argento:* i.e., made in the same clay.

670. *qua cava sunt:* i.e., on the inside. Wooden cups were so treated to stop the drink seeping into the wood itself.

671. *foci misere:* 'the hearth (*foci*, plur. for sing.) provided (lit. 'sent forth')'. *Epulas* refers to the food already mentioned in lines 647–50.

672. *nec:* the negative belongs to *longae*, not to the verb: 'and wines of no great age'. Vintage wines would naturally be beyond the means of Ph. and B., who were content with ordinary *vins du pays*.

    rursus referuntur: 'the wine (*vina*, plur. for sing.) is brought back again'. Presumably, then, though we have not been told so, they had drunk during the *parva mora* (l. 671).

677f. *vultus . . . voluntas:* lit. 'there were in addition kindly faces, and goodwill (which was) not feeble and scant'.

detulit et minuit parvoque admovit aeno, 645
quodque suus coniunx riguo collegerat horto,
truncat holus foliis; furca levat ille bicorni
sordida terga suis nigro pendentia tigno
servatoque diu resecat de tergore partem
exiguam sectamque domat ferventibus undis. . . .

In lines 651–9 (omitted) Philemon and Baucis give
their guests water to wash with, and get ready a
simple couch for them to recline on, in Roman
fashion. Philemon and Baucis prepare and serve
a simple country meal (660–78).

Accubuere dei. Mensam succincta tremensque 660
ponit anus, mensae sed erat pes tertius impar:
testa parem fecit; quae postquam subdita clivum
sustulit, aequatam mentae tersere virentes.
Ponitur hic bicolor sincerae baca Minervae
conditaque in liquida corna autumnalia faece 665
intibaque et radix et lactis massa coacti
ovaque non acri leviter versata favilla,
omnia fictilibus. Post haec caelatus eodem
sistitur argento crater fabricataque fago
pocula, qua cava sunt, flaventibus illita ceris; 670
parva mora est, epulasque foci misere calentes,
nec longae rursus referuntur vina senectae
dantque locum mensis, paulum seducta, secundis:
hic nux, hic mixta est rugosis carica palmis
prunaque et in patulis redolentia mala canistris 675
et de purpureis collectae vitibus uvae,
candidus in medio favus est; super omnia, vultus
accessere boni nec iners pauperque voluntas.

679. *repleri:* inf. dep., like *succrescere*, on *vident*.

680. *per se = sponte sua*, 'of itself'.

681. *supinis:* i.e., thrown back above the shoulders with the palms turned upwards (which ancient art shows was the regular gesture of prayer.).

683. *nullis paratibus:* i.e., the fact that they'd made no preparations but had had to improvise.

684. *minimae custodia villae: custodia*, abstract for concrete. The word *villa*, which denotes the country resort of a wealthy Roman, is used here to make the same point as was made by *eodem argento* in l. 668f.

685. *dis hospitibus:* 'the gods of hospitality'.
   domini: 'the owners (of the goose)'.

686. *tardos aetate:* 'slow with age', referring to Ph. and B.

688. *necari:* sc. *anserem* as subj.

689. *-que:* connecting *dixerunt* in the next line with *vetuere* in the prec. line: 'they forbade (the goose) to be killed, and said "we are gods, and . . ." '. Cp. l. 717.

690f. *vobis dabitur:* join these two words in tr. *mali* is gen. after *immunibus*.

693. *simul:* sc. *nobiscum*.

695. *summo:* sc. *clivo*.
   semel: 'in one flight'.

698. *suorum:* i.e., of their neighbours.

699. Tr. in the foll. order: *illa vetus casa, parva etiam duobus dominis*.

700. *furcas:* the word may be used of anything fork-shaped: here of the gable of Ph. and B.'s cottage.

The gods reveal their identity; they take Philemon and Baucis up to a high hill, flood the impious neighbourhood, and turn the cottage into a temple (679–702).

Interea totiens haustum cratera repleri
sponte sua, per seque vident succrescere vina: 680
attoniti novitate pavent manibusque supinis
concipiunt Baucisque preces timidusque Philemon
et veniam dapibus nullisque paratibus orant.
Unicus anser erat, minimae custodia villae:
quem dis hospitibus domini mactare parabant;   685
ille celer penna tardos aetate fatigat
eluditque diu tandemque est visus ad ipsos
confugisse deos: superi vetuere necari,
'Di' que 'sumus, meritasque luet vicinia poenas
impia,' dixerunt; 'vobis immunibus huius   690
esse mali dabitur; modo vestra relinquite tecta
ac nostros comitate gradus et in ardua montis
ite simul!' Parent ambo baculisque levati
nituntur longo vestigia ponere clivo.
Tantum aberant summo, quantum semel ire sagitta   695
missa potest: flexere oculos et mersa palude
cetera prospiciunt, tantum sua tecta manere,
dumque ea mirantur, dum deflent fata suorum,
illa vetus dominis etiam casa parva duobus
vertitur in templum: furcas subiere columnae,   700
stramina flavescunt aurataque tecta videntur
caelataeque fores adopertaque marmore tellus.

Jupiter asks Philemon and Baucis what prayer they would like to make, and they ask that they should be allowed to be the guardians of the

703. *Saturnius:* 'son of Saturn', i.e., Jupiter.

706. *iudicium commune:* 'their joint decision'.

709. *auferat . . . videam . . . sim:* subjunctives expressing wish.

711. *tutela:* abstract for concrete: 'they were the guardians of the temple'.

712. *soluti:* 'weakened'.

713. *locique narrarent casus:* lit. 'and were talking about the events of the place', i.e., about how their cottage had been changed into a temple. It is appropriate that the second metamorphosis should occur as they are reminiscing about the first one.

716. *geminos vultus:* 'both their faces'. Cp. *de gemino corpore*, l. 720.

719. *Thyneius:* 'of Bithynia', in Asia Minor.

720. *vicinos truncos:* The oak and the linden-tree (see Introd.).

721. *neque . . . vellent:* lit. 'nor was there (a reason) why they should want to deceive me'.

723. *recentia:* sc. *serta*.

    dixi: the subject is Lelex, who is telling this tale.

724. *cura:* abstract for concrete, with *deum* (= *deorum*) as objective gen. Tr. 'those who cared for the gods'.

    colantur: sc. *ei* as subject, and antecedent to *qui*.

temple, and that they should both die on the same day. These requests are granted, and after their death the couple are turned into trees (703–24).

Talia tum placido Saturnius edidit ore:
'Dicite, iuste senex et femina coniuge iusto
digna, quid optetis.' Cum Baucide pauca locutus   705
iudicium superis aperit commune Philemon:
'Esse sacerdotes delubraque vestra tueri
poscimus, et quoniam concordes egimus annos,
auferat hora duos eadem, nec coniugis umquam
busta meae videam, neu sim tumulandus ab illa.'   710
Vota fides sequitur: templi tutela fuere,
donec vita data est; annis aevoque soluti
ante gradus sacros cum starent forte locique
narrarent casus, frondere Philemona Baucis,
Baucida conspexit senior frondere Philemon.   715
Iamque super geminos crescente cacumine vultus
mutua, dum licuit, reddebant dicta 'Vale' que
'O coniunx' dixere simul, simul abdita texit
ora frutex; ostendit adhuc Thyneius illic
incola de gemino vicinos corpore truncos.   720
Haec mihi non vani (neque erat, cur fallere vellent)
narravere senes; equidem pendentia vidi
serta super ramos ponensque recentia dixi
'Cura deum di sunt, et, qui coluere, colantur.'

7

Orpheus and Eurydice

INTRODUCTION TO 'ORPHEUS AND EURYDICE'

This, like 'Proserpina' (No. 5), is the story of a quest, this time for a lost wife. A folk-tale, known from Thrace to North America and Japan, tells how a husband went to the other world to fetch his wife, and lost her because he broke some taboo. Naturally enough there are taboos attached to the well-nigh impossible task of getting people back from the dead: Proserpina ate some pomegranate seeds and thereby broke the taboo about not eating food there; in consequence she could only return for a part of the year. The taboo in the Orpheus story, that men must avert their eyes from gods or ghosts of the underworld, is also widespread (in the Old Testament, God says 'No man may look upon me and live').

In the Sixth book of Virgil's *Aeneid*, the Sybil tells the Trojan hero Aeneas: 'to go *down* to the world of the dead is easy; it's *getting back* that's difficult'. Hamlet calls Death:

> That undiscovered country, from whose bourne
> No traveller returns.

Death stands close behind us all, and is both certain and final (32–6, below). The story of Orpheus and Eurydice is the expression, in myth, of men's knowledge of death's finality.

Orpheus himself figures in myth as a famous musician and singer. When he played his lyre and sang, all nature listened, and wild beasts were tamed (cp. 40–6). He is the personification of the power of music, which has always been experienced as uncanny. Milton's bestial wizard,

Comus, when he hears the virtuous Lady singing, exclaims:

> Such sober certainty of waking bliss
> I never heard till now.

But even Orpheus, for all the combination of his love and musical power, cannot overcome Death.

Virgil, at the end of his *Georgics*, also tells this story. He dwells more on the pathos of the situation: he pictures Orpheus wandering on the shore, singing from dawn till sundown. Ovid dismisses this aspect in a business-like line and a bit (11f.). Virgil also makes more of the drama inherent in the tale (see on l. 57). Both these points illuminate the difference between the two poets.

NOTES TO
'ORPHEUS AND EURYDICE'

2. *Hymenaeus:* the god of marriage, Hymen.

    Ciconum (gen.) : the Cicones were a Thracian tribe who lived near the river Hebrus.

3. *Orphea . . . vocatur:* lit. 'was summoned in vain by the voice of Orpheus'. *nequiquam:* because Orpheus' marriage led to disaster rather than happiness.

7. *nullosque . . . ignes:* lit. 'found no fires by its movements', i.e., it was shaken, but would not burst into flame and so provide a good omen.

8. *exitus auspicio gravior:* a compressed phrase: 'the outcome (of the wedding) was worse than the omen (indicated)'.

8f. *nupta . . . nova:* 'the bride' ('newly-wed').

11. *quam:* the antecedent is *nupta nova*, i.e., Eurydice. Take *postquam* next in translation.

    Rhodopeius . . . vates: 'the bard of Rhodope', Orpheus. Rhodope, a mountain range in Thrace (l. 77), is made to stand for Thrace as a whole, the home of O.

12. *ne . . . umbras:* lit. 'lest he should not also make trial of the shades', i.e. 'in order to include the underworld in his search'.

13. *Styga:* the *Styx* was the river in Hades which the spirits of the dead had to cross in order to reach their appointed place. If their bodies had not received proper burial, they were forbidden to cross it.

    Taenaria porta (abl.) : at Taenarum, 75 km. from Sparta, there is a famous rift in the rock-strata, which was thought to be an entrance to Hades.

14. *leves:* 'light', i.e., phantom.

    simulacra functa sepulcro: lit. 'shades (which had) finished with the tomb', i.e., ghosts whose bodies had received proper burial.

16. *ad:* 'in accompaniment to' his songs.

19. *falsi . . . oris:* lit. 'the circumlocutions of a false mouth having been laid aside', i.e., 'in sincere and plain speech'.

Book 10

7. ORPHEUS AND EURYDICE

Eurydice, Orpheus' new bride, dies from snake-bite (1-10). Orpheus goes down to the Under-world and pleads with Pluto and Persephone to allow her back to the Upper World (11-39).

Inde per immensum croceo velatus amictu
aethera digreditur Ciconumque Hymenaeus ad oras
tendit et Orphea nequiquam voce vocatur.
Adfuit ille quidem, sed nec sollemnia verba
nec laetos vultus nec felix attulit omen.   5
Fax, quoque, quam tenuit, lacrimoso stridula fumo
usque fuit nullosque invenit motibus ignes.
Exitus auspicio gravior: nam nupta per herbas
dum nova naiadum turba comitata vagatur,
occidit in talum serpentis dente recepto.   10
Quam satis ad superas postquam Rhodopeius auras
deflevit vates, ne non temptaret et umbras,
ad Styga Taenaria est ausus descendere porta
perque leves populos simulacraque functa sepulcro
Persephonen adiit inamoenaque regna tenentem   15
umbrarum dominum pulsisque ad carmina nervis
sic ait: 'O positi sub terra numina mundi,
in quem recidimus, quicquid mortale creamur,
si licet et falsi positis ambagibus oris
vera loqui sinitis, non huc, ut opaca viderem   20

21f. *uti . . . monstri:* lit. 'in order that I might bind the three throats (sc. necks) of the Medusaean monster', in preparation for hauling him up out of Hades as Hercules did. The 'Medusaean monster' is Cerberus, the three-headed watchdog of Hades, whose hair was composed of snakes.

25. *posse pati volui:* lit. 'I wished to have the power to endure (my loss)'.

    Temptasse: sc. *pati.*

26. *deus hic:* 'this God', i.e., Amor.

27. *an sit et hic:* indirect question dep. on *dubito:* 'I don't know whether he (the god of Love) is (well known) here (in Hades) too'. Supply *bene notum* again with *esse.*

28. *rapinae:* refers to Pluto's theft of Proserpina.

29. *vos:* i.e., Pluto and Proserpina.

36. *haec quoque:* 'she also', Eurydice.

    cum . . . annos: lit. 'when she will have passed through the years which are allotted to her (*iustos*) and will be ripe (i.e., ready for death)'.

37. *iuris erit vestri:* lit. 'will be of (i.e., subject to) your jurisdiction'.

    pro munere poscimus usum: lit. 'I ask (*poscimus* plur. for sing.) for enjoyment (of her) as a gift (from you)'.

38f. *certum . . . mihi:* lit. 'I am resolved (*certum est mihi*) to refuse (*nolle*) to return (to the world of the living)'.

41ff. *Tantalus*, etc.: these are all ghosts who are undergoing punishment in the underworld; while they hear the sound of the lyre the punishment ceases.

45f. *tunc . . . genas:* take *fama est* first in translating. Lit. 'the story goes that then first the cheeks of the Eumenides, conquered by (the beauty of) the song, grew wet with tears'.

46f. *nec . . . negare: sustinet* is here followed by the inf. *negare:* lit. 'neither does the royal wife (Proserpina) take it upon herself to say no to her entreaties (*oranti*, lit. 'to her entreating'), not (does Pluto) who rules the Lower World *ima*)'.

48. *Eurydicen:* Greek acc. *illa* refers to Eurydice.

Tartara, descendi, nec uti villosa colubris
terna Medusaei vincirem guttura monstri:
causa viae est coniunx, in quam calcata venenum
vipera diffudit crescentesque abstulit annos.
Posse pati volui nec me temptasse negabo: 25
vicit Amor. Supera deus hic bene notus in ora est;
an sit et hic, dubito; sed et hic tamen auguror esse,
famaque si veteris non est mentita rapinae,
vos quoque iunxit Amor. Per ego haec loca plena
per Chaos hoc ingens vastique silentia regni,   [timoris, 30
Eurydices, oro, properata retexite fata.
Omnia debemur vobis, paulumque morati
serius aut citius sedem properamus ad unam.
Tendimus huc omnes, haec est domus ultima, vosque
humani generis longissima regna tenetis.   35
Haec quoque, cum iustos matura peregerit annos,
iuris erit vestri: pro munere poscimus usum;
quodsi fata negant veniam pro coniuge, certum est
nolle redire mihi: leto gaudete duorum.'

> His plea is granted on condition that he does not
> look back at Eurydice until they reach the Upper
> World (40–52); he breaks the condition and she
> returns to Hades (53–63).

Talia dicentem nervosque ad verba moventem   40
exsangues flebant animae; nec Tantalus undam
captavit refugam, stupuitque Ixionis orbis,
nec carpsere iecur volucres, urnisque vacarunt
Belides, inque tuo sedisti, Sisyphe, saxo.
Tunc primum lacrimis victarum carmine fama est   45
Eumenidum maduisse genas, nec regia coniunx
sustinet oranti nec, qui regit ima, negare,
Eurydicenque vocant: umbras erat illa recentes

49. *inter:* this prep. is here in retarded position, but governs *umbras* just the same.

> *de:* 'from', 'as a result of'.

50. *hanc simul et legem:* lit. 'Orpheus received her (his wife) and at the same time a condition (*legem*)'.

51. *Avernas:* adj. 'of Avernus', i.e., 'of the Underworld', *pars pro toto*, Avernus being a lake *in* the Underworld.

52. *aut ... futura* (sc. *esse*): 'otherwise the gift (*dona*, plur. for sing.) would be null and void'.

55. *āfuērŭnt:* scanned as three long syllables, the *u* sounding like an English 'w'. Otherwise the word would not fit into an hexameter line, since it contains a cretic (— *v* —).

56. *ne deficeret metuens: metuens* here governs the fearing clause *ne deficeret*.

57. Ovid dismisses in one line the great dramatic climax of the story. Virgil, with surer dramatic sense (or more self-identified with Orpheus), tells how 'sudden madness' seized O.:

> Pardonable, you'd say, but Death can never pardon.
> He halts. Eurydice, his own, is now on the lip of
> Daylight. Alas! he forgot. His purpose broke. He
>   looked back.
> His labour was lost, the pact he had made with the
>   merciless king.
> Annulled. Three times did thunder peal over the pools
>   of Avernus. (Tr. by C. Day Lewis)

61. *quereretur:* 'for what was she to complain of, except the fact that she was beloved?' O.'s disastrous action had been due to his great love for her (l. 56).

74. *Cereris munere:* 'the gift of Ceres', i.e., bread.

75. I.e., he fed on grief and tears instead of bread.

77. *Haemum:* Mt. Haemus was another high mountain in Thrace.

inter et incessit passu de vulnere tardo.
Hanc simul et legem Rhodopeius accipit Orpheus,   50
ne flectat retro sua lumina, donec Avernas
exierit valles; aut irrita dona futura.
Carpitur acclivis per muta silentia trames,
arduus, obscurus, caligine densus opaca,
nec procul afuerunt telluris margine summae;   55
hic, ne deficeret, metuens avidusque videndi
flexit amans oculos, et protinus illa relapsa est.
Bracchiaque intendens prendique et prendere certans
nil nisi cedentes infelix arripit auras,
iamque iterum moriens non est de coniuge quicquam   60
questa suo (quid enim nisi se quereretur amatam?)
supremumque 'Vale', quod iam vix auribus ille
acciperet, dixit revolutaque rursus eodem est. . . .

Lines 54–71 (omitted) contain some irrelevant
mythology.
Orpheus grieves for Eurydice for a week by the
river Styx, and then returns to Thrace (72–7).

Orantem frustraque iterum transire volentem
portitor arcuerat; septem tamen ille diebus
squalidus in ripa Cereris sine munere sedit;
cura dolorque animi lacrimaeque alimenta fuere.   75
Esse deos Erebi crudeles questus, in altam
se recepit Rhodopen pulsumque aquilonibus Haemum.

8

Pygmalion

INTRODUCTION TO 'PYGMALION'

Pygmalion was king of Cyprus. This story about his statue coming to life is well known today because of Bernard Shaw's play *Pygmalion*, about a Professor Higgins who takes a flower-girl from Covent Garden and makes her into a lady, and then falls in love with her. Ovid's version of the tale is the best we have from antiquity. It is a local legend, originating in the fact that the master-craftsman (Daedalus is another case), like the master-musician (Orpheus), seemed to possess magical powers in his ability to make Art rival, and indeed to excel Nature. Pygmalion falls in love with his statue *because* it is more beautiful than any real woman could be (l. 248f.).

The theme of Art excelling Nature was a favourite one with the Romantics and with Shakespeare. When, in *Antony and Cleopatra*, Enobarbus is trying to convey to his hearers the surpassing beauty of Cleopatra, he describes her as:

> O'er-picturing that Venus where we see
> The fancy outwork Nature.

That is, the painting of a Venus by a great painter is more beautiful than any mortal woman can be, but Cleopatra was, *per impossibile*, more beautiful still.

Ovid, typically, sees the humorous side of the situation, especially in the first half. Pygmalion is afraid of bruising the statue by squeezing it too hard (l. 257f.), and gives her head a soft pillow to rest on, 'as though she could feel it' (*tamquam sensura*, l. 269). The account of the metamorphosis itself is one of the best in the whole of the *Metamorphoses*.

The description of the statue growing warm (281) and soft like wax in the sun (283–6), of the blood beginning to flow (289), and finally of the decorous maidenly blush as she opens her eyes (293f.), is skilfully interwoven with the description of Pygmalion's reactions—his first excited hopes (281f.), incredulous joy (287f.), and outburst of gratitude to Venus before he falls to kissing again. The incident was well suited to the genius of the author of the *Ars Amatoria* (see Introd.).

NOTES TO 'PYGMALION'

247. *feliciter:* lit. 'with happy result'. Cp. the English word 'felicitously'.

248. *sculpsit:* the subject is Pygmalion.

249. *concepit amorem:* lit. 'he conceived love of (+gen)', he fell in love with.

251. Lit. 'and (you would think) that she wanted to move, if modesty did not prevent her'. Cp. Shakespeare's Desdemona, who was 'so still and quiet, that her motion blushed at her self'.

252. *ars . . . sua* (abl.)*:* lit. 'so hidden is the skill by its own skill'. The statue was the product of a skill so unobtrusive as not to be noticed.

253. *ignes:* plur. for sing., 'the fire of love', for the counterfeit body.

254. *an sit:* sc. 'to find out' as introducing this indirect question.

258. Tr. in the order *metuit, ne livor veniat.*

263. *Heliadum* (gen.)*:* the Heliades were the daughters of the sun-god Helios and therefore sisters of Phaethon. For their 'tears' of amber, see No. 3, 'Phaethon', lines 364–6, with notes.

265. *aure:* '*from* her ear', but *pectore:* '*on* her breast'.

267. *hanc:* the statue. *concha Sidonide:* 'purple from Sidon'.

269. *sensura* (sc. *plumas*)*:* agreeing with *colla.*

Book 10

8. PYGMALION

Pygmalion carves a statue so beautiful that he falls in love with it (247–69).

Interea niveum mira feliciter arte
Sculpsit ebur formamque dedit, qua femina nasci
nulla potest, operisque sui concepit amorem.
Virginis est verae facies, quam vivere credas,   250
et, si non obstet reverentia, velle moveri:
ars adeo latet arte sua. Miratur et haurit
pectore Pygmalion simulati corporis ignes.
Saepe manus operi temptantes admovet, an sit
corpus an illud ebur, nec adhuc ebur esse fatetur.   255
Oscula dat reddique putat loquiturque tenetque
et credit tactis digitos insidere membris
et metuit, pressos veniat ne livor in artus,
et modo blanditias adhibet, modo grata puellis
munera fert illi conchas teretesque lapillos   260
et parvas volucres et flores mille colorum
liliaque pictasque pilas et ab arbore lapsas
Heliadum lacrimas; ornat quoque vestibus artus,
dat digitis gemmas, dat longa monilia collo;
aure leves bacae, redimicula pectore pendent: 265
cuncta decent; nec nuda minus formosa videtur.
Collocat hanc stratis concha Sidonide tinctis
appellatque tori sociam acclinataque colla
mollibus in plumis, tamquam sensura, reponit.

(111)

270. *Cypro* (abl.): from *Cyprus* (fem.), the island.

271. *aurum*: retained acc. See on No. 4, l. 97.

272. *nivea cervice*: locative abl., '*on* their white necks'.

274. *constitit*: the subject is *Pygmalion* (l. 276).

275f. *mea* (276) goes with *coniunx* (275). To ask for the statue to come alive would have been blasphemous: the nearest thing to that was to ask *sit coniunx mea similis eburnae* (*virgini*), 'may I have a wife *like* this ivory maiden'. But Venus understood what he really wanted.

277. *sensit*: supply *Venus* as subj. from the foll. clause.

278. *vota . . . velint*: indirect question with *quid* postponed, the clause introduced by *sensit* in the prec. line: '(Venus) realized what that prayer (*vota*, plur. for sing.) meant'.

    omen: acc. in apposition to the sentence contained in the next line.

279. *accensa est*: 'flared up'. Contrast the way Orpheus' wedding torches *fail* to catch alight and thereby afford a *bad* omen (No. 7, 'Orpheus and Eurydice', l. 6f.).

280. *simulacra*: plur. for sing.

281. *visa tepere est*: sc. *puella* as subj.

282. *pectora*: plur. for sing. (contrast *pectore*, l. 265).

283. *posito rigore*: abl. absolute, lit. 'its hardness having been laid aside'. The phrase repeats the idea of *mollescit* by stating its opposite. 'At his touch the ivory lost its hardness and grew soft' (Innes).

286. *ipso usu*: 'by actual use'.

288. *sua vota*: abstract for concrete, '(the object of) his hopes'.

290f. *plenissima concipit verba*: 'thinks of a wealth of words'.

293. *ad lumina lumen*: Ovid is playing on the two senses of the word *lumen*: *lumina* means 'the daylight' and *lumen* 'her eyes'.

290. *Paphius heros*: 'the hero of Paphos', Pygmalion. Paphos was actually a town *in* Cyprus, but the two names are used interchangeably (see below, l. 297).

295. *coactis . . . orbem*: Lit. 'the horns of the moon having been forced nine times into full orb', i.e., after nine full moons, the period of gestation.

At the festival of Venus, Pygmalion prays to the goddess that his statue should really live (270–6). His prayer is granted, and his statue becomes his wife, and gives birth to Paphos (276–97).

Festa dies Veneris tota celeberrima Cypro   270
venerat, et pandis inductae cornibus aurum
conciderant ictae nivea cervice iuvencae,
turaque fumabant, cum munere functus ad aras
constitit et timide 'Si, di, dare cuncta potestis,
sit coniunx, opto,' non ausus 'eburnea virgo'   275
dicere, Pygmalion 'similis mea' dixit 'eburnae'.
Sensit, ut ipsa suis aderat Venus aurea festis,
vota quid illa velint, et, amici numinis omen,
flamma ter accensa est apicemque per aera duxit.
Ut rediit, simulacra suae petit ille puellae   280
incumbensque toro dedit oscula; visa tepere est;
admovet os iterum, manibus quoque pectora temptat:
temptatum mollescit ebur positoque rigore
subsidit digitis, ceditque, ut Hymettia sole
cera remollescit tractataque pollice multas   285
flectitur in facies ipsoque fit utilis usu.
Dum stupet et dubie gaudet fallique veretur,
rursus amans rursusque manu sua vota retractat.
Corpus erat! Saliunt temptatae pollice venae.
Tum vero Paphius plenissima concipit heros   290
verba, quibus Veneri grates agat, oraque tandem
ore suo non falsa premit, dataque oscula virgo
sensit et erubuit timidumque ad lumina lumen
attollens pariter cum caelo vidit amantem.
Coniugio, quod fecit, adest dea, iamque coactis   295
cornibus in plenum noviens lunaribus orbem
illa Paphon genuit, de qua tenet insula nomen.

9

Midas

INTRODUCTION TO 'MIDAS'

Old Silenus, tutor and companion of Bacchus, was captured by Phrygian peasants and taken to their king, Midas. Midas recognized him, held a festival in his honour, and then returned him safely to Bacchus. Bacchus, in gratitude to Midas, offered to grant him anything he might choose.

The story of Midas takes us back to the world of moralistic fairy-tale to which 'Philemon and Baucis' (No. 6) belonged, where wine is miraculously renewed, cottages turn into temples, and people into trees. Its moral is the same as that of 'Phaethon' (No. 3), that people are apt to choose silly things, and that if they do they must take the consequences. Midas, being a grown man, had less excuse than Phaethon, and his choice is wicked rather than merely silly, because it is the result of avarice. It is the necessary outcome of his evil character just as the choice of Philemon and Baucis reflected their true piety. Midas' story is different, however, in that he is given a miraculous *power*. In this respect it is like H. G. Wells' story, *The Man Who Could Work Miracles*, which also has the moral that it is not good for a mere man to be granted superhuman powers.

The moral aspect is stressed by Ovid as it was in 'Philemon and Baucis'. Midas acknowledges that his choice was an evil one (*peccavimus*, l. 132). Bacchus also emphasizes his guilt (*male optato*, l. 136), and grants him absolution after he has done penance (134–41). The last part of this story, about Midas washing in the river Pactolus, must have arisen, partly at any rate, to explain the golden look of the sands of that river.

The story of Midas getting asses' ears because of his stupidity is like a famous modern fairy-tale—Pinocchio. Pinocchio, after his visit to the island of pleasure, had his ears turned into those of an ass, and narrowly escaped a total transformation; and his nose got longer every time he told a lie. In the fairy-tale world, the outward shape is liable to be altered to suit the inward disposition.

NOTES TO 'MIDAS'

100. *Huic:* Midas. *deus:* Bacchus.

100f. *optandi muneris arbitrium:* 'the power of choosing a gift'.

101. *altore:* i.e., Silenus.

103. *vertatur:* consecutive subjunctive without *ut*, foll. *effice*. The indefinite (*quicquid*) clause acts as subj.

104. *optatis:* dat. after *adnuit*, 'his wishes'.

    munera solvit: solvo here bears its sense of *fulfilling an obligation.* Lit. 'he paid the (promised) gift' (*munera* plur. for sing.).

105. *Liber:* subj. of the sentence. Another name for Bacchus.

106. *Berecynthius heros:* 'the hero of Berecynthus' is Midas, because he was the son of Cybele, who was worshipped on Mt. Berecynthus in Phrygia.

107. *polliciti fidem:* 'the reliability of the promise'.

108. *sibi:* dat. after *credens*, i.e., the evidence of his own senses. *Credens* applies in time to the whole of this and the next line.

    non alta: must agree, despite its position, with *ilice* and not with *fronde*: the tree was low enough for Midas to be able to break off a branch.

    fronde virentem: take together, agreeing with *virgam*.

111. *contactu potenti:* causal abl., 'by the power of his touch'.

112. *arentis:* acc. plur. *Cereris:* i.e., of corn.

114. *Hesperidas:* because golden apples grew in the garden of the Hesperides.

117. *palmis:* abl. of separation, 'flowing off his hands'.

    Danaen eludere posset: another learned reference. Danae the mother of Perseus was visited by Jupiter in the form of a shower of golden rain.

118. I.e., his hopes outstripped the power of his imagination.

    fingens: sc. *animo*, 'imagining'.

119. *gaudenti:* sc. *ei*. Lit. 'for him rejoicing'. Tr. 'So he exulted in his good fortune, while servants set before him . . .' (Innes).

120. *tostae frugis:* lit. 'baked corn', i.e., bread.

121. *sua:* scan the line!

    Cerealia (adj.): 'of Ceres' (cp. *Cereris*, l. 112).

Book 11

9. MIDAS

Midas asks that anything he touches may turn to
gold, but discovers the snags when it comes to
mealtimes (100–26).

Huic deus optandi gratum, sed inutile fecit   100
muneris arbitrium, gaudens altore recepto.
Ille male usurus donis ait 'Effice, quicquid
corpore contigero, fulvum vertatur in aurum.'
Adnuit optatis nocituraque munera solvit
Liber et indoluit, quod non meliora petisset.   105
Laetus abit gaudetque malo Berecynthius heros
pollicitique fidem tangendo singula temptat
vixque sibi credens, non alta fronde virentem
ilice detraxit virgam; virga aurea facta est;
tollit humo saxum: saxum quoque palluit auro;   110
contigit et glaebam: contactu glaeba potenti
massa fit; arentis Cereris decerpsit aristas:
aurea messis erat; demptum tenet arbore pomum:
Hesperidas donasse putes; si postibus altis
admovit digitos, postes radiare videntur;   115
ille etiam liquidis palmas ubi laverat undis,
unda fluens palmis Danaen eludere posset;
vix spes ipse suas animo capit aurea fingens
omnia. Gaudenti mensas posuere ministri
exstructas dapibus nec tostae frugis egentes: 120
tum, vero, sive ille sua Cerealia dextra

124. *premebat:* here 'covered'.
125. *auctorem muneris:* 'the donor of the gift', Bacchus, i.e., wine.
126. *rictus:* plur. for sing.

129. *copia:* sc. *cibi.*
130. *meritus:* ptcpl. from *mereor:* lit. 'having deserved (his fate)'.
132. *Lenaee:* epithet for Bacchus, taken from the Greek word for a wine-press.
133. *eripe:* sc. *me.*
134. *deum = deorum:* mite: sc. *est.*
   pecasse = peccavisse, inf. after *fatentem.*
135. *pacti fide* (abl.) *data* (acc.): 'given in fulfilment of his promise'.
   solvit: here 'cancelled' (contrast l. 104 above).
136. *male optato auro:* 'the gold, an evil wish'.
137. *Sardibus:* dat. after *vicinum.* Sardis was the ancient capital of Lydia, just north of Mt. Tmolus.
   amnem: the river Pactolus.
138. *per iugum Lydum:* with *labentibus* rather than with *carpe viam,* 'through the Lydian mountain range'.
139. *carpe viam:* 'make your way', 'keep going'.
140. *qua plurimus exit:* 'where its outflow is most abundant'.
141. *exue crimen:* 'free yourself from guilt simultaneously (with immersing yourself in the stream)'. Cp. the Christian rite of baptism, and see Introd. to this piece.
142. *iussae:* '(which he had been) bidden (to approach)'.
144. *iam veteris* (venae): because a long time has intervened since Bacchus's original gift.
   venae: gen. dep. on *semine.*

munera contigerat, Cerealia dona rigebant,
sive dapes avido convellere dente parabat,
lammina fulva dapes admoto dente premebat;
miscuerat puris auctorem muneris undis: 125
fusile per rictus aurum fluitare videres.

When Midas repents, Bacchus revokes the gift,
and tells him to wash in the river Pactolus, the sands
of which have been golden ever since (127–45).

Attonitus novitate mali divesque miserque
effugere optat opes et quae modo voverat, odit.
Copia nulla famem relevat; sitis arida guttur
urit, et inviso meritus torquetur ab auro   130
ad caelumque manus et splendida bracchia tollens
'Da veniam, Lenaee pater! Peccavimus' inquit,
'sed miserere, precor, speciosoque eripe damno!'
Mite deum numen: Bacchus peccasse fatentem
restituit pactique fide data munera solvit   135
'Neve male optato maneas circumlitus auro,
vade,' ait 'ad magnis vicinum Sardibus amnem
perque iugum Lydum labentibus obvius undis
carpe viam, donec venias ad fluminis ortus,
spumigeroque tuum fonti, qua plurimus exit,   140
subde caput corpusque simul, simul exue crimen.'
Rex iussae succedit aquae: vis aurea tinxit
flumen et humano de corpore cessit in amnem;
nunc quoque iam veteris percepto semine venae
arva rigent auro madidis pallentia glaebis. . . .   145

Lines 146–71 (omitted) tell how Pan and Apollo
engage in a contest to prove which of them is the
better musician. The judge, Timolus, the moun-
tain-god, decides in favour of Apollo.

172. *-que*: joins *iudicium* with the whole phrase *sancti sententia montis*.

174. *Delius*: Apollo, because the island of Delos was his birthplace.

176. *trahit in spatium*: i.e. he makes them longer.

177. *dat posse moveri*: lit. 'gives (them) the power (*posse*) to be moved', i.e. to swing about as human ears cannot.

178. *partem damnatur in unam*: lit. 'he is penalised with respect to just one part'.

179. *induitur*: pass. used like the Greek middle voice: 'he wears'.

    lente gradientis: this is what is called an 'ornate' epithet, having no special relevance to the context but being universally applicable to all asses.

180. *celare*: sc. *aures*.

    turpis pudore: lit. 'disgraced with shame'.

184. *cupiens efferre sub auras*: this participial clause is best tr. after the second *nec* clause which begins in the next line.

    Efferre sub auras means 'to bring out into the open air'.

186. *domini quales aspexerit aures*: indirect question dep. on *refert* in the next line.

187. *terrae haustae*: 'the earth he had dug up'.

188. *tellure regesta*: abl. absolute.

191. *pleno anno*: 'when the year was full', i.e. at harvest time.

192. *agricolam*: 'the farmer', i.e. the man who had dug the hole and planted his words like seeds.

Midas disputes the decision and Apollo punishes him by changing his ears into those of an ass. Midas wears a turban to conceal them, but his barber finds out, and not daring to reveal the truth openly, but unable to keep silence altogether, digs a hole in the ground and whispers the secret into the hole (172–89).

Iudicium sanctique placet sententia montis
omnibus, arguitur tamen atque iniusta vocatur
unius sermone Midae; nec Delius aures
humanam stolidas patitur retinere figuram,   175
sed trahit in spatium villisque albentibus implet
instabilesque imas facit et dat posse moveri:
cetera sunt hominis, partem damnatur in unam
induiturque aures lente gradientis aselli.
Ille quidem celare cupit turpisque pudore   180
tempora purpureis temptat velare tiaris;
sed solitus longos ferro resecare capillos
viderat hoc famulus, qui cum nec prodere visum
dedecus auderet, cupiens efferre sub auras,
nec posset reticere tamen, secedit humumque   185
effodit et, domini quales aspexerit aures,
voce refert parva terraeque immurmurat haustae
indiciumque suae vocis tellure regesta
obruit et scrobibus tacitus discedit opertis.

Reeds grow up over the spot, and whenever the wind blows through them, they whisper the words of the barber (190–3).

Creber harundinibus tremulis ibi surgere lucus   190
coepit et, ut primum pleno maturuit anno,
prodidit agricolam: leni iam motus ab austro
obruta verba refert dominique coarguit aures.

Vocabulary

A

abdo, –ere, –idi, –itum—hide.

abeo, –ire, –ii, –itum—go away.

abluo, –ere, –ui, –ūtum—wash away, purify.

absum, –esse, –āfui—be absent.

absumo, –ere, –mpsi, –mptum—take away.

accedo, –ere, –cessi, –cessum—approach, be added.

accendo, –ere, –ndi, –nsum—kindle, set on fire.

accensus, –ūs, (m)—a kindling, setting on fire.

accingo, –ere, –nxi, –nctum—gird on, surround.

accipio, –ere, –cēpi, –ceptum—receive, hear.

acclinatus, –a, –um—reclining.

acclīvis, –e—ascending, steep.

accommodo (1)—fit, adapt.

accumbo, –ere, –cubui, –cubitum—lie down, recline at table.

aciēs, ēi, (f)—point, sharp edge, line of battle.

acūtus, –a, –um—sharp.

ad (prep. with acc.)—to, towards, at, by, in accompaniment.

addo, –ere, –didi, –ditum—add to, bring to.

adeo (adv.)—to such an extent.

adhibeo, –ere, –ui, –itum—use, employ.

adhūc (adv.)—hitherto, still, even now.

adimo, –ere, –ēmi, –emptum—take away, deprive.

adiuvo, –are, –iūvi, –iūtum—help.

admiror, (1 dep.)—wonder, be surprised.

admissus, –a, –um—quickened.

admoveo, –ere, –mōvi, –mōtum—bring near, apply.

adnuo, –ere, –nui, –nūtum—agree to, grant (with dat.).

adoperio, –ire, –vi, –tum—cover over.

adsum, –esse, –fui—be present, aid.

aduncus, –a, –um—hooked.

aduro, –ere, –ussi, –ustum—burn.

adversus, –a, –um—in front of, opposite, opposed.

adveho, –ere, –vexi, –vectum—carry, bring.

aedes, –is, (f)—building, house, temple.

aemulus, –a, –um—striving to imitate.

aenum, –i, (n)—bronze pot.

aequālis, –e—equal.

aequātus, –a, –um—level.

aequē (adv.)—in like manner, equally.

aequor, –oris, (n)—sea.

aequus, –a, –um—level, equal, smooth, fair, just.

āēr, āeris, (m)—air.

aes, aeris, (n)—bronze, (plur.) cymbals.

aestuo, (1)—rage, burn.

aestus, –ūs, (m)—heat.

aetas, –ātis, (f)—age.

aeternus, –a, –um—eternal.

aether, –eris, acc. aethera (m)—upper air, heaven.

aetherius, –a, –um—heavenly, of heaven.

aevum, –i, (n)—age, lifetime.

affecto, (1)—claim, strive after.

afflo, (1)—blow on, breathe on.

ager, –ri, (m)—field.

agito, (1)—drive, shake, disturb.

agna, –ae, (f)—ewe lamb.

agnosco, –ere, –nōvi, –nitum—recognize.

ago, –ere, –ēgi, –actum—drive, pass (life), act.

agricola, –ae, (m)—farmer, sower.

aio, ait, (defective)—say.

āla, –ae, (f)—wing.

albeo, –ere—be white.

albesco, –ere—become white.

albus, –a, –um—white.

āles, –itis, (f)—bird.

alimenta, –orum, (n. pl.)—food, nourishment.

ālipēs, –edis—with wings on the feet, swift-footed.
aliquis, –quid—anyone, someone.
aliter, (adv.)—otherwise, differently.
alligo, (1)—bind, fasten.
almus, –a, –um—(lit.) nourishing, kindly.
alnus, –i, (f)—alder tree.
alter, –tera, –terum—the one, the other, (of two).
altor, –oris, (m)—tutor, foster-father.
altus, –a, –um—high, deep.
ambāges, –is (f)—a roundabout way.
ambiguum, –i, (n)—doubt, uncertainty.
ambo, –ae, –o—both.
ambrosia, –ae, (f)—ointment of the gods.
ambūro, –ere, –ussi, –ustum—scorch, burn round.
āmentia, –ae, (f)—madness.
amīcus, –a, –um—friendly, loving.
amictus, –ūs, (m)—cloak.
amnis, –is, (m)—river.
amo, (1)—love.
amor, –ōris, (m)—love.
amplexus, –ūs, (m)—embrace.
an (conj.)—whether.
anhēlitus, –ūs, (m)—breath, panting.
anīlis, –e—of an old woman.
anima, –ae, (f)—life, breath, soul.
annus, –i, (m)—year.
anser, –eris, (m)—goose.
ante, (prep. with acc.)—before; (adv.)—formerly, before.
antrum, –i, (n)—cave.
anus, –ūs, (f)—old woman.
aperio, –ire, –erui, –ertum—open, reveal.
apex, –icis, (m)—highest point (of a flame).
appello, (1)—call.
appōno, –ere, –posui, –positum—place before.
apto, (1)—fit, apply.
aptus, –a, –um—apt, suitable; (with dat.) suitable for.

aqua, –ae, (f)—water.
aquila, –ae, (f)—eagle.
aquilo, –ōnis, (m)—north wind.
aquōsus, –a, –um—rainy, moist, watery.
arātor, –ōris, (m)—ploughman.
arātrum, –i, (n)—plough.
arbitrium, –i, (n)—judgement, will, power.
arbor, –oris, (f)—tree.
arboreus, –a, –um—of a tree.
arbuteus, –a, –um—of the strawberry tree.
arceo, –ere, –ui, –ctum—ward off.
arctus, –i, acc. arcton—north pole.
arcus, –ūs, (m)—bow, bow shape.
ardeo, –ere, –arsi, –arsum—catch fire, burn.
arduus, –a, –um—lofty, steep.
āreo, (2)—be dry.
ārens, –ntis—dry.
argentum, –i, (n)—silver.
arguo, –ere, –ui, –ūtum—question.
aridus, –a, –um—dry.
arista, –ae, (f)—ear of corn.
armentum, –i, (n)—herd.
arripio, –ere, –ui, –eptum—seize, snatch.
ars, artis, (f)—skill, art.
artus, –uum, (m. pl.)—limbs.
arvum, –i, (n)—ploughed field.
asellus, –i, (m)—a little ass.
asper, –era, –erum—rough.
aspergo, –inis, (f)—sprinkling, spray.
aspicio, –ere, –spexi, –spectum—look at, see.
assuētus, –a, –um—accustomed.
asto, –are, –stiti—stand near.
āter, ātra, ātrum—black, dark.
attollo, –ere, (no perf. or supine)—raise, lift up.
attonitus, –a, –um—astonished.
auctor, –ōris, (m)—author, adviser.

audax, –cis,—bold.
audeo, –ere, ausus sum—dare.
aufero, –ferre, abstuli, ablatum—take away, carry off.
auguror, (1 dep.)—guess, surmise.
aura, –ae, (f))—air, (also plu.)
aurātus, –a, –um—golden.
aureus, –a, –um—golden.
aurīga, –ae, (m)—charioteer.
auris, –is, (f)—ear.
aurum, –i, (n)—gold.
auspicium, –i, (n)—omen.
auster, –tri, (m)—south wind.
austrālis, –e—southern.
ausum, –i, (n)—daring attempt, undertaking.
autumnālis, –e—autumnal.
avēna, –ae, (f)—oats, any grain, a shepherd's reed-pipe.
aversor, (1 dep.)—turn away from, drive away.
avidus, –a, –um—greedy, hungry.
avis, –is, (f)—bird.
āvius, –a, –um—remote, untrodden, pathless.

B
bāca, –ae, (f)—berry, fruit, pearl.
baculum, –i, (n)—stick.
bicolor, –oris—two-coloured.
bicornis, –e—two-horned, two-pronged.
blanditia, –ae, (f)—flattery, (plur.) endearments.
blandus, –a, –um—flattering, pleasant, agreeable.
boreas, –ae, (m)—north wind.
bōs, bovis, (c)—bull, cow.
brevis, –e—short.
bracchium, –i, (n)—arm, branch.
bustum, –i, (n)—usually plur.—tomb.
buxus, –i, (f)—the box-tree.

C

cacūmen, –inis, (n)—tree-top, top end.

cado, –ere, cecidi, cāsum—fall, be killed.

cādūcifer, –fera, –ferum—carrying the caducus, the symbol of the god Mercury.

caecus, –a, –um—blind.

caedes, –is, (f)—slaughter, blood.

caedo, –ere, cecīdi, caesum—cut down, kill.

caelātus, –a, –um—chased, embossed.

caelestis, –e—heavenly. In plur., the gods.

caelicola, –ae, (c)—deity, god.

caelum, –i, (n)—sky, heaven.

caeruleus, –a, –um—blue.

calathus, –i, (m)—basket.

calco (1)—tread upon.

caleo, –ere, –ui—be warm.

calidus, –a, –um—warm, hot.

cālīgo, –inis, (f)—darkness.

callidus, –a, –um—clever, shrewd, experienced.

calor, –ōris, (m)—heat.

campus, –i, (m)—field, plain.

candesco, –ere, –ui—become white, begin to glow.

candidus, –a, –um—white, shining.

candor, –ōris, (m)—whiteness, brilliance.

cāneo, –ere, –ui—grow white.

canistrum, –i, (n)—basket.

canna, –ae, (f)—reed, cane.

cano, –ere, cecini, cantum—sing, proclaim, sound.

cantus, –ūs, (m)—song, incantation.

cānus, –a, –um—white.

capillus, –i, (m)—hair.

capio, –ere, cēpi, captum—capture, take, contain.

captīvus, –i, (m)—prisoner.

capto, (1)—try to catch, snatch.

caput, –itis, (n)—head.

carbasus, –i, (f), plur. carbasa (n)—linen, linen garment.

carcer, –eris, (m)—prison, the starting-point of a race.
cardo, –inis, (m)—hinge.
careo, (2), (with abl.)—lack, be in need of.
cārica, –ae, (f)—a dried fig.
carmen, –inis, (n)—song, poetic inscription.
carpo, –ere, –psi, –ptum—(trans.) pluck; (intrans.) travel.
cārus, –a, –um—dear.
casa, –ae, (f)—cottage.
cāsus, –ūs, (m)—event, chance, misfortune.
cauda, –ae, (f)—tail.
causa, –ae, (f)—cause, reason.
caveo, –ere, cāvi, cautum—take care, decree.
caverna, –ae, (f)—cave, grotto.
cavus, –a, –um—hollow.
cēdo, –ere, cessi, cessum—yield, retire, (with dat.) yield to.
celeber, celebris, –bre—famous, much frequented.
celebro, (1)—throng, haunt, hold, celebrate.
celer, celeris, –ere—swift.
cēlo, (1)—hide.
celsus, –a, –um—tall lofty.
censeo, (2)—judge, decree.
cēra, –ae, (f)—wax.
cerno, –ere, crēvi, crētum—see, perceive.
certo, (1)—fight; (with infin.) strive.
certus, –a, –um—certain, unmistakable.
cerva, –ae, (f)—female deer.
cervix, –icis, (f)—neck.
cesso (1)—be inactive, give up.
cēteri, –ae, –a—other (people or things).
ceu (adv.)—as if, just as.
cibus, –i, (m)—food.
cingo, –ere, –nxi, –nctum—surround, gird.
cinis, –eris, (m)—ash.
circumlino, –linere, no perf., –litum—smear all over.
cithara, –ae, (f)—lyre.
citius (comp. adv.)—sooner.

citrā (prep.)—on this side of.

citus, -a, -um—swift.

clāmo, (1)—shout; (with acc.) call to.

clārus, -a, -um—famous; (of sound) loud.

claudo, -ere, -si, -sum—shut.

clīvus, -i, (m)—hill, slope.

coarguo, -ere, -ui—prove, demonstrate, publish.

coctilis, -e—burned; with muri, built of burned bricks.

coeo, -ire, -ivi or -ii, -itum—come together.

coepi, -isse, -ptum (def.)—begin.

coerceo, (2)—enclose, confine, constrain.

cognosco, -ere, -nōvi, -nitum—get to know, recognize.

cōgo, -ere, -egi, -actum—force, collect, thicken, curdle.

colligo, -ere, -lēgi, -lectum—collect, gather, pick.

collūceo, (2)—shine.

collum, -i, (n), often plur.—neck.

colo, -ere, -ui, cultum—cultivate, live in, worship.

colōnus, -i, (m)—farmer, settler.

color, -ōris, (m)—colour.

coluber, -ri, (m)—serpent.

columba, -ae, (f)—dove.

columna, -ae, (f)—pillar.

coma, -ae, (f)—hair, leaf.

comes, -itis, (m)—companion, comrade.

comitātus, -a, -um—accompanied, attended.

commentus, -a, -um—so-called, bogus.

comminus, (adv.)—at close quarters, near at hand.

committo, -ere, -mīsi, -missum—entrust, commit.

commūnis, -e—common, mutual; (with dat.) common to.

compesco, -ere, -ui—confine; (sitim.) slake, quench.

complector, -i, -plexus—embrace.

complexus, -ūs, (m)—embrace.

compōno, -ere, -posui, -positum—lay to rest (trans.).

comprendo, -ere, -di, -sum—seize, grasp.

concavo, (1)—curve (into a concave shape).

concentus, ūs, (m)—harmony.

concha, –ae, (f)—shell, trumpet, purple-fish.
concipio, –ere, –cēpi, –ceptum—receive, conceive, design.
concordo, (1)—agree, unite.
concors, concordis—in harmony, together.
concutio, –ere, –cussi, –cussum—shake.
condicio, –ōnis, (f)—condition.
condo, –ere, –didi, –ditum—hide, store.
confīne, –is, (n)—boundary, borderland.
confiteor, –eri, –fessus—confess, acknowledge.
confugio, –ere, –fūgi—flee, take refuge.
coniugium, –i, (n)—union, marriage.
coniunx, –iugis, (c)—husband, wife.
cōnor, (1 dep.)—try.
conprecor, (1 dep.)—pray.
conscius, –a, –um—conscious, privy to.
conscius, –i, (m)—accomplice, confidant.
consenesco, –ere, –senui—grow old.
consilium, –i, (n)—plan, advice.
consisto, –ere, –stiti, –stitum—halt, remain, stand.
consulo, –ere, –ui, –ultum—consult; (with dat.) look after.
consūmo, –ere, –mpsi, –mptum—eat, consume.
contactus, –ūs, (m)—touch.
contendo, –ere, –tendi, –tentum—strive.
contemptor, –ōris, (m)—despiser.
contentus, –a, –um—satisfied.
conterminus, –a, –um—neighbouring, near to.
contiguus, –a, –um—next, touching, neighbouring.
contingo, –ere, –tigi, –tactum—touch, reach.
cōnūbium, –i, (n)—marriage.
convello, –ere, –velli, –vulsum—tear, shake.
convenio, –ire, –vēni, –ventum—come together, fit.
cōpia, –ae, (f)—plenty, wealth, supply, opportunity.
cornū, –ūs, (n)—horn, end, tip.
cornus, –i, (f)—cornel-tree.
corōna, –ae, (f)—crown, wreath.
corōno, (1)—crown, wreath, surround.

corrigo, –ere, –rexi, –rectum—set right, smooth out.
corripio, –ere, –ui, –eptum—snatch, seize.
cortex, –icis, (m)—bark, rind.
crātēr, ēris, acc. –ēram, (m)—mixing-bowl for wine.
crēber, –bra, –brum—thick, frequent.
crēdo, –ere, –didi, –ditum—think, believe; (with dat.) trust.
cremo, (1)—burn.
creo, (1)—make, create.
crepito, (1)—rattle, clatter.
cresco, –ere, crēvi, crētum—grow, increase.
crīmen, –inis, (n)—crime, accusation, judgement.
crīnālis, –e—pertaining to the hair.
crīnis, –is, (m)—hair; (usually plur.).
croceus, –a, –um—saffron-coloured, yellow.
crocum, –i, (n), and crocus, –i, (m)—saffron flower.
cruentātus, –a, –um—bloodstained.
cruentus, –a, –um—bloody, murderous.
cruor, –ōris, (m)—blood, bloodshed.
crūs, crūris, (n)—leg.
culpo, (1)—blame.
cunctus, –a, –um—all, all together, the whole.
cupīdo, –inis, (f)—desire, eagerness.
cupidus, –a, –um—desirous, eager, greedy.
cupio, –ere, –ii, –itum—wish, want, desire.
cūra, –ae, (f)—care, anxiety.
cūro, (1)—look after, take care of.
curro, –ere, cucurri, cursum—run.
currus, –ūs, (m)—chariot.
cursus, –ūs, (m)—race, running, course.
curvāmen, –inis, (n)—bend, curve.
curvātus, –a, –um, and curvus, –a, –um—bent, curved.
cuspis, –idis, (f)—point; (II 199) the sting of a scorpion.
custōdia, –ae, (f)—protection.
custos, –ōdis, (c)—watchman, guardian.
cycnus, –i, (m)—swan.

D

damno, (1)—blame, condemn.

damnōsus, –a, –um—injurious, hurtful.

damnum, –i, (n)—loss, damage, harm.

dapes, fem. plur.—meal.

dea, –ae, (f)—goddess.

debeo, (2)—ought, owe.

decens, –ntis—seemly, beautiful.

dēcerpo, –ere, –psi, –ptum—pluck.

dēcido, –ere, –cidi—fall down.

dēclīno, (1)—turn aside.

dēclīve, –is (n)—a downward slope.

dēclīvis, –e—sloping downwards.

decor, (m), and decus, (n), –ōris—beauty, grace, dignity.

dēdecus, –ōris, (n)—disgrace, shame.

dēfero, –ferre, –tuli, –lātum—bring.

dēficio, –ere, –fēci, –fectum—fail (in strength or quantity).

dēfleo, –ere, –flēvi, –flētum—weep for, mourn.

dēlābor, –i, –lapsus sum—fall down, glide down.

dēlūbrum, –i, (n)—temple, shrine.

dēmissus, –a, –um—let down, cast down.

dēmitto, –ere, –mīsi, –missum—send down, drive down.

dēmo, –ere, –mpsi, –mptum—take away.

dēnique (adv.)—at last.

dens, –ntis, (m)—tooth.

densus, –a, –um—thick.

dēpōno, –ere, –posui, –positum—put down; (sitim.) slake, quench.

dēpositum, –i, (n)—anything entrusted for safe keeping, a trust.

dēprecor, (1 dep.)—pray (esp. for the averting of evil).

dēprendo, –ere, –di, –sum—catch.

dēscendo, –ere, –i, –nsum—descend.

dēsero, –ere, –ui, –sertum—desert, leave.

dēsino, –ere, –ii—stop, leave off.

dēsuētus, –a, –um—unaccustomed.

dētineo, –ere, –ui, –tentum—keep back, detain.
deus, –i, (m)—god.
dēvoveo, –ere, –vōvi, –vōtum—vow, devote, sacrifice.
dexter, –era, –erum—right (hand, side).
dīco, –ere, dixi, dictum—say.
dictum, –i, (n)—word.
diēs, –ēi, (m., sing. also f)—day, light of day.
diffundo, –ere, –fūdi, –fūsum—pour out, scatter.
digitus, –i, (m)—finger, toe.
dignus, –a, –um (with abl.)—worthy.
dīgredior, –i, –gressus—go away.
diligo, –ere, –lexi, –lectum—love.
dīmoveo, –ere, –mōvi, –mōtum—remove.
dīrectus, –a, –um—straight.
discēdo, –ere, –cessi, –cessum—go away.
discidium, –i, (n)—separation.
dispar, –aris—unlike, different.
dispicio, –ere, –spexi, –spectum—see through, discern.
dissuādeo, –ere,– –si, –sum—dissuade.
diū (adv.)—for a long time.
dīva, –ae, (f)—goddess.
dīvello, –ere, –velli, –vulsum—tear apart.
dīversus, –a, –um—different, contrary.
dīves, –itis—rich.
dīvido, –ere, –vīsi, –vīsum—divide.
do, dare, dedi, datum—give.
doceo, –ere, –ui, doctum—teach, tell.
dolor, –ōris, (m)—pain, grief.
domina, –ae, (f)—mistress.
dominus, –i, (m)—master.
domo, –are, –ui, –itum—tame.
domus, –i, (f)—house, home.
dōnec (conj.)—until.
dōnum, –i, (n)—gift.
dōs, dōtis, (f)—dowry.
dryades, –um, (f pl.)—wood-nymphs.

dubito, (1)—doubt, wonder, hesitate.
dubius, –a, –um—uncertain.
dūco, –ere, duxi, ductum—lead; (lanas) spin; (rimam)
  receive, acquire.
dummodo (conj.)—provided that.
dūrus, –a, –um—hard.
duo, duae, duo—two.
dux, –cis, (m)—leader.

E

ebur, –oris, (n)—ivory; (IV 148) ivory scabbard.
eburneus, –a, –um—made of ivory.
ecce!—behold!
ēdo, –ere, –didi, –ditum—bring forth, tell, utter.
ēdūco, –ere, –duxi, –ductum—lead out.
effero, –ferre, extuli, ēlatum—bring out, lift.
efficio, –ere, –fēci, –fectum—cause, bring about, make.
effluo, –ere, –fluxi—flow out.
effodio, –ere, –fōdi, –fossum—dig out.
effugio, –ere, –fūgi—flee, escape.
effulgeo, –ere, –fulsi—shine forth, gleam.
egeo, –ere, –ui, (with gen.)—need, lack.
ēgredior, –i, –gressus—go out.
ēiaculor (1 dep.)—throw out.
ēiecto (1)—throw out.
electrum, –i, (n)—amber; (plur.) drops of amber gum.
ēlūdo, –ere, –si, –sum—frustrate, elude.
ēminus (adv.)—from a distance.
ēmico, –are, –ui, –atum—rush forth, shoot out.
ēmitto, –ere, –mīsi, –missum—send out.
ēn!—look, behold!
ēnītor, –i, –nisus, or nixus—climb.
ensis, –is, (m)—sword.
eo, ire, ii, itum—go.
epulae, –arum, (f. pl.)—feast, meal.
equidem (adv.)—indeed, in truth.

equus, –i, (m)—horse.

ērigo, –ere, –rexi, –rectum—raise, build; (oculos) open.

ēripio, –ere, –ui, –eptum—snatch away.

ergo (adv.)—so, therefore.

erro (1)—wander.

ērubesco, –ere, erubui—grow red.

ērudio, (4)—teach, educate.

etiamnum (adv.)—even now.

ēvādo, –ere, –si, –sum—escape.

ēvānesco, –ere, evānui—vanish.

eventus, –ūs, (m)—result.

exaudio (4)—listen.

excēdo, –ere, –cessi, –cessum—go away.

excido, –ere, –cidi—(with abl.) fall from, fail in.

excipio, –ere, –cēpi, –ceptum—take, capture, receive, follow after.

exclāmo (1)—shout.

excutio, –ere, –cussi, –cussum—shake.

exeo, –ire, –ii, –itum—go out; (trans.) leave.

exhaurio, –ire, –hausi, –haustum—endure, drain.

exhorresco, –ere, –rui—tremble, shudder.

exigo, –ere, ēgi, –actum—drive out, finish.

exiguus, –a, –um—small.

exitus, ūs, (m)—escape, result.

expallesco, –ere, –pallui—turn pale.

expers, –rtis (with gen.)—taking no thought for.

expertus, –a, –um—skilled, experienced.

exsanguis, –e—bloodless.

exsisto, –ere, –stiti, –stitum—arise.

exspatior, (1)—wander from the course.

exspiro, (1)—breathe out.

extemplo (adv.)—immediately.

extendo, –ere, –di, –tum—stretch out.

extinguo, –ere, –nxi, –nctum—extinguish, kill.

extrēmus, –a, –um—last; extrema luna—the setting moon.

extruo, –ere, –xi, –uctum—build up.

exuo, –ere, –ui, –utum—put off, strip.
exuviae, –arum (f. plur.)—spoils, trophies.

F

fabrico, (1)—make, carve.
fābula, –ae, (f)—story.
facies, –ēi, (f)—face, form, condition, appearance.
facio, –ere, fēci, factum—make, do.
faex, –cis, (f)—sediment, lees, the brine of pickles.
fāgus, –i, (f)—beech-tree, beech-wood.
fallo, –ere, fefelli, falsum—deceive, trick.
falsus, –a, –um—false, decitful.
fāma, –ae, (f)—fame, rumour, story.
fames, –is, (f)—hunger.
famula, –ae, (f)—maidservant.
famulus, –i, (m)—manservant.
fateor, –eri, fessus—confess, acknowledge.
fatīgo, (1)—tire, exhaust.
fātum, –i, (n)—fate.
favilla, –ae, (f)—glowing ashes, embers.
favor, –ōris, (m)—favour, goodwill.
favus, –i, (m)—honey-comb.
fax, facis, (f)—torch.
fēcundus, –a, –um—fruitful, rich.
fēmina, –ae, (f)—woman, wife.
fera, –ae, (f)—wild beast.
ferīnus, –a, –um—wild.
fero, ferre, tuli, latum—bear, carry, endure.
feror (passive of fero)—go, move.
ferrūgo, –inis, (f)—lit. iron-rust; any dark colour.
ferrum, –i, (n)—sword.
fertilitas, –tātis, (f)—fruitfulness, fertility.
ferus, –a, –um—wild, savage.
fervens, –ntis—hot, warm, burning, glowing, boiling.
ferveo, –ere, ferbui—boil.
festum, –i, (n)—festival.

fētus, –ūs, (m)—fruit, produce.
fictilia, –ium, (n. plur.)—earthenware vessels.
fides, –ei, (f)—faith, fulfilment, promise, credibility.
fīdus, –a, –um—faithful; (with dat.) faithful to.
fīgo, –ere, fixi, fixum—fix, transfix, imprint.
figūra, –ae, (f)—form, shape.
fīlia, –ae, (f)—daughter.
fīlius, –i, (m)—son.
fīlum, –i, (n)—thread.
findo, –ere, fidi, fissum—split.
fingo, –ere, finxi, fictum—shape, form, imagine.
fīnio, (4)—finish.
fīnis, –is, (m)—end, goal; in plur. boundaries.
fissus, –a, –um (past part. of findo)—split, separated,
    divided.
fistula, –ae, (f)—water-pipe, reed-pipe.
flāgro, (1)—burn.
flāmen, –inis, (n)—blowing (especially of wind; usu. plur.)
flamma, –ae, (f)—flame.
flammifer, –fera, –ferum—flame-bearing.
flāveo, –ere—be yellow.
flāvesco, –ere—become yellow.
flāvus, –a, –um—yellow.
flecto, –ere, –flexi, –flexum—turn aside, bend.
fleo, –ere, flēvi, flētum—weep; (trans.) weep for.
flētus, –ūs, (m)—weeping, tears.
flexus, –ūs, (m)—bend, curve.
flōs, flōris, (m)—flower.
fluito, (1)—flow.
flūmen, –inis, (n)—river.
fluo, –ere, fluxi, fluxum—flow.
focus, –i, (m)—hearth.
foedus, –eris, (n)—treaty, agreement.
folium, –i, (n)—leaf.
fons, –ntis, (m)—fountain.
forāmen, –inis, (n)—opening, aperture.

fores, –um, (f plur.)—doors.
forma, –ae, (f)—shape, beauty.
formīdo, –inis, (f)—fear, terror.
formosus, –a, –um—beautiful.
fornax, –cis, (f)—furnace, oven.
fors, –rtis, (f)—chance, luck.
forsitan (adv.)—perhaps.
fortē (adv.)—by chance, as it happened.
fortis, –e—strong, brave.
fortūna, –ae, (f)—fate, luck, fortune.
fossa, –ae, (f)—ditch.
frāga, –orum (n. plur.)—strawberries.
frāter, –tris, (m)—brother.
frāternus, –a, –um—belonging to a brother, brotherly.
frēna, –orum, (n. plur.)—bridle, curb; (of a boat) rudder.
frequento, (1)—celebrate, attend (in great numbers).
frētus, –a, –um (with abl.)—relying on.
frīgus, –oris, (n)—cold.
frondens, –ntis—leafy.
frondesco, –ere—put forth leaves, shoot.
frons, –dis, (f)—leaf, foliage.
frons, –ntis, (f)—forehead, brow, facial expression.
frūges, –um, (f. plur.)—crops.
frustrā (adv.)—in vain.
frutex, –icis, (m)—bark of a tree.
frux, –gis, (f), usually plur.—fruits of the earth, crops.
fuga, –ae, (f)—flight.
fugax, –cis—fleeing, fugitive.
fugio, –ere, fūgi, fugitum—flee.
fugo, (1)—put to flight.
fulica, –ae, (f)—water-fowl, coot.
fulgeo, –ere, fulsi—shine, glitter.
fulgor, –oris, (m)—brightness, splendour.
fulmen, –inis, (n)—thunderbolt.
fulvus, –a, –um—golden, yellow.
fūmidus, –a, –um—smoky.

fūmo, (1)—smoke.

fūmus, –i, (m)—smoke, steam.

fungor, –im, functus—perform, discharge, have done with (with abl.).

furca, –ae, (f)—fork.

furiālis, –e—raging.

furtum, –i, (n)—theft, robbery.

fūsilis, –e—liquid.

G

galea, –ae, (f)—helmet.

gaudeo, –ere, gāvīsus (semi-dep.)—rejoice; (with abl.) rejoice in.

gelidus, –a, –um—very cold, icy.

geminus, –a, –um—twin, two, twofold.

gemitus, –ūs, (m)—groan, lamentation.

gemma, –ae, (f)—gem, jewel.

gena, –ae, (f)—cheek.

gener, –eri, (m)—son-in-law.

genetrix, –icis, (f)—mother.

genitor, –ōris, (m)—parent, father, sire.

gens, –ntis, (f)—race, tribe.

genū, –ūs, (n)—knee.

genus, –eris, (n)—birth, origin.

gero, –ere, gessi, gestum—do, wear.

gesto, (1)—carry, have, wear.

gestio, (4)—to desire.

gigno, –ere, genui, genitum—beget, bear.

glaeba, –ae, (f)—clod of earth.

glans, –ndis, (f)—acorn.

gradior, –i, gressus—walk.

gradus, –ūs, (m)—step.

grāmen, –inis, (n)—grass.

grānum, –i, (n)—grain, seed.

grātes, (f. plur.)—thanks.

grātia, –ae, (f)—favour, regard, influence.

grātus, –a, –um—pleasing.
gravidus, –a, –um—pregnant.
gravis, –e—heavy, stern.
gravitas, –tātis, (f)—weight, dignity, sternness.
gravo, (1)—burden, weigh down.
grex, gregis, (m)—herd, flock.
gurges, –itis, (m)—lit. whirlpool; pool, sea.
gutta, –ae, (f)—drop.
guttur, –uris, (n)—throat, gullet.

H

habēna, –ae, (f)—thong, strap; (plur.) reins.
habeo, (2)—have, hold, consider.
habitābilis, –e—habitable.
habito, (1)—inhabit, dwell.
haereo, –ere, –si, –sum—stick fast, cling, hesitate; (with
   dat.) cling to, stick to.
harēna, –ae, (f)—sand.
harundo, –inis, (f)—reed, cane.
hasta, –ae, (f)—spear.
haurio, –ire, hausi, haustum—draw up or out; drink, drain,
   empty, absorb.
haustus, –us, (m)—draught, drink.
habeto, (1)—make blunt, make dim.
hedera, –ae, (f)—ivy.
herba, –ae, (f)—grass, springing vegetation, green crops.
heros, –ōis, (m)—hero, demigod.
hesternus, –a, –um—of yesterday.
hinc (adv.)—from here; Hinc . . . illinc—on this side . . .
   . . . on that side.
hinnītus, –ūs, (m)—neighing.
holus, –eris, (n)—cabbage.
honor, or honos, –ōris, (m)—honour, prize.
hōra, –ae, (f)—hour.
horrendus, –a, –um—fearful, terrifying, horrible.
horridus, –a, –um—rough, uncouth.

hortus, –i, (m)—garden.
hospes, –itis, (m) ⎱
hospita, –ae, (f) ⎰—host, guest, foreigner.
hostis, –is, (c)—enemy.
huc (adv.)—hither.
hūmānus, –a, –um—human.
humilis, –e—low, humble.
humus, –i, (m)—ground, soil.

I

iaceo, (2)—lie down; (of the face) cast down, drooping.
iacio, –ere, iēci, iactum—throw; (of seed) sow.
iacto, (1)—throw, aim.
iactūra, –ae, (f)—loss.
iaculor (1 dep.)—hurl, throw.
iamdūdum—already for some time.
ibi (adv.)—there.
ictus, –ūs, (n)—blow, striking, impac.
īdem, eadem, idem (pron.)—the same.
ideo (adv.)—for that reason, therefore.
iecur, iecoris, (n)—liver.
iēiūnium, –i, (n), usually plur.—fasting, hunger.
ignārus, –a, –um—ignorant, unaware.
ignifer, –a, –um—fire-bearing.
ignis, –is, (m)—fire.
ignosco, –ere, –nōvi, –nōtum (with dat.)—pardon.
ignōtus, –a, –um—unknown.
īlex, –icis, (f)—holm-oak, ilex.
īlium, –i, (n)—usually plur.—side of the body, flank.
illic (adv.)—there.
illinc (adv.)—from there, on that side.
illino, –ere, –lēvi, –litum—smear, coat.
illustris, –e—clear, bright.
imber, –bris, (m)—rain, shower, storm.
imitor, (1 dep.)—copy, imitate.
immemor, –oris, (with gen.)—forgetful, forgetting.

immineo, (2)—be near to, threaten (by nearness).
immītis, –e—harsh, cruel, stern.
immūnis, –e—safe, untouched; (with gen.) free from.
immurmuro, (1)—whisper into (with dat.)
impar, –aris—unequal, unmatched.
impatiens, –ntis—impatient, not able to bear something, intolerant.
impedio, (4)—hinder, prevent.
impello, –ere, –puli, –pulsum—drive, set in motion.
imperfectus, –a, –um—unfinished, incomplete.
impero, (1)—order, demand.
impetūs, –us, (m)—attack, force, speed.
impietas, –tātis, (f)—irreverence, impiety.
impius, –a, –um—wicked.
impleo, –ere, –ēvi, –ētum—fill.
impōno, –ere, –posui, –positum—put.
īmus, –a, –um—lowest.
inamoenus, –a, –um—unpleasant, gloomy.
inānis, –e—empty, useless.
inarātus, –a, –um—unploughed.
incēdo, –ere, –cessi, –cessum—walk.
incendium, –i, (n)—fire.
inclūdo, –ere, –si, –sum—shut in, confine, imprison.
incola, –ae, (c)—inhabitant, peasant.
increpo, (1)—make a noise, chide, blame.
incresco, –ere, –crēvi—grow, increase.
incumbo, –ere, –cubui, –cubitum—fall upon, rush towards.
incurso, (1)—rush upon, charge.
inde (adv.)—from there.
indicium, –i, (n)—evidence, trace.
indigena, –ae (adj.)—native, indigenous.
indignor (1 dep.)—consider unworthy.
indignus, –a, –um—unworthy, not deserving.
indolesco, –ere, –lui—grieve.
indūco, –ere, –xi, –ctum—lead in, overlay, spread over.
induo, –ere, –ui, ūtum—put on.

iners, –ertis—inert, sluggish, passive.
inexpugnābilis, –e—impregnable, that cannot be rooted out.
infectus, –a, –um—unfinished.
infēlix, –icis—unhappy, unfortunate.
inferior, –ius—lower.
infernus, –a, –um—underground, belonging to the lower regions.
infractus, –a, –um—discordant.
ingens, –ntis—huge.
ingrātus, –a, –um—ungrateful.
inhibeo, (2)—check, restrain.
inīquus, –a, –um—unfair, hostile, discontented.
iniūria, –ae, (f)—wrong, injury.
innītor, –i, –nixus—lean upon.
innubus, –a, –um—unwedded.
innuptus, –a, –um—unwedded.
inops, –opis—helpless; (with gen.) without.
inornātus, –a, –um—unadorned, unbound (of hair).
inquīro, –ere, –sīvi, –sītum—search for, inquire.
insānus, –a, –um—mad.
inscius, –a, –um—not knowing, ignorant.
insequor, –i, –sectūs—follow, pursue.
insero, –ere, –ui, –sertum—bring into, join.
insido, –ere, –sēdi, –sessum—sink into (with dat.).
instabilis, –e—unstable, shaky, fickle.
instar, (n. indecl.)—(with gen.) like, resembling.
insula, –ae, (f)—island.
intactus, –a, –um—untouched.
intempestīvus, –a, –um—untimely, inopportune.
intendo, –ere, –di, –tum—stretch out.
intereā (adv.)—meanwhile.
interdum (adv.)—from time to time.
interritus, –a, –um—undaunted, undismayed.
intibum, –i, (n)—endive.
intonsus, –a, –um—unshaven.

intrēmo, –ere, –ui—tremble, shake.
intro (1)—enter.
intus (adv.)—within.
inūtilis, –e—useless.
invenio, –ire, –vēni, –ventum—find.
inventum, –i, (n)—device, invention.
invideo, –ere, –vīdi, –vīsum—grudge, be jealous.
invidiōsus, –a, –um—full of resentment.
invidus, –a, –um—envious, churlish.
invītus, –a, –um—unwilling.
involvo, –ere, –vi, –ūtum—roll upon, wrap around.
īra, –ae, (f)—anger.
īrascor, –i, –rātus—be angry; (with dat.) be angry with.
īrātus, –a, –um—angry.
irrequiētus, –a, –um—unquiet, restless.
irritus, –a, –um—vain, useless.
iste, –a, –ud—that (demonstrative pronoun).
iter, itineris, (n)—road, way, course.
iterum (adv.)—again.
iuba, –ae, (f)—mane.
iubeo, –ere, iussi, iussum—order, command.
iūdex, –icis, (m)—judge.
iūdicium, –i, (n)—judgement, decision.
iugum, –i, (n)—yoke; mountain range.
iungo, –ere, –nxi, –nctum—join.
iūro, (1)—swear.
iūs, iūris, (n)—law, justice, duty.
iussum, –i, (n)—command.
iustus, –a, –um—just, upright, due.
iuvenālis, –e—youthful, of young men.
iuvenca, –ae, (f)—heifer.
iuvenis, –is, (m)—young man.
iuvo, –are, iūvi, iūtum—help.

L

labo, (1)—totter, slip, toss about.

lābor, –i, lapsus—glide, flow smoothly.
labor, –ōris, (m)—labour, toil, work.
lac, lactis, (m)—milk.
lacertus, –i, (m)—arm.
lacrima, –ae, (f)—tear.
lacrimōsus, –a, –um—tearful, causing tears.
laedo, –ere, laesi, laesum—hurt, wound.
laetus, –a, –um—joyful.
laevus, –a, –um—left, on the left side.
lammina, –ae, (f)—thin piece of wood or metal.
lampas, –adis, (f)—torch, oil-lamp.
lāna, –ae, (f)—wool (also plur.)
lanio, (1)—tear in pieces, rend.
lapillus, –i, (m)—little stone, pebble, jewel.
lapis, –idis, (m)—stone.
lassus, –a, –um—tired.
latebra, –ae, (f)—(usually plur.) hiding-place.
lateo, –ere, –ui—lurk, lie concealed.
latito, (1)—hide (intrans.).
lātus, –a, –um—broad, wide.
latus, –eris, (n)—side, flank.
laudo, (1)—praise.
laurus, –i, (f)—laurel.
laus, –dis, (f)—praise, fame.
lavo, –ere, lāvi, lautum—wash.
lea, –ae, (f)—lioness.
leaena, –ae, (f)—lioness.
lego, –ere, lēgi, lectum—gather, read.
lēnis, –e—gentle.
lentē (adv.)—slowly.
leo, –ōnis, (m)—lion.
lepus, –oris, (m)—hare.
lētum, –i, (n)—death.
levis, –e—light, inconstant, easy to bear.
levitas, –tātis, (f)—light-mindedness, inconstancy.
levo, (1)—raise, relieve, support.

lex, lēgis, (f)—law, condition.
liber, –era, –erum—free.
liber, libri, (m)—bark of a tree.
lībo, (1)—pour out, make a libation.
lībro, (1)—balance, poise (a dart or javelin).
licet, –cuit or licitum est (impers.)—it is permitted.
lignum, –i, (n)—wood, firewood.
līlium, –i, (n)—lily.
limbus, –i, (m)—border, hem.
līmes, –itis, (m)—route.
lingua, –ae, (f)—tongue.
līnum, –i, (n)—flax, linen.
liquidus, –a, –um—liquid.
lītus, –oris, (n)—beach, shore.
līvor, –ōris, (m)—bluish colour (of bruises).
lolium, –ī, (n)—darnel.
longus, –a, –um—long, long-lasting.
loquor, –i, locūtus—speak.
lōrum, –i, (n)—thong, (in plur.) reins.
lūceo, –ere, luxi—become light, shine.
lūcidus, –a, –um—bright, shining.
luctūs, –us, (m)—sorrow, distress.
lūcus, –i, (m)—grove, thicket.
lūdo, –ere, –si, –sum—play.
lūgeo, –ere, –xi, –ctum—mourn.
lūmen, –inis, (n)—light, eye.
lūna, –ae, (f)—moon.
lūnāris, –e—of the moon.
luo, –ere, –ui—(poenas) suffer punishment.
lupus, –i, (m)—wolf.
lustro, (1)—purify, wander over.
lūsus, –ūs, (m)—game.
lux, –ūcis, (f)—light, daylight.
lymphātus, –a, –um—crazy.
lyra, –ae, (f)—lyre, lute.

M

macto, (1)—sacrifice.
madefacio, –ere, –fēci, –fectum—moisten, make wet.
madeo, –ere, –ui—be wet.
madidus, –a, –um—wet.
maestus, –a, –um—sad, mournful.
magnus, –a, –um—large, great.
male (adv.)—wrongly, wickedly.
mālo, malle, mālui—prefer.
malus, –a, –um—bad, evil.
mando, (1)—entrust, order.
māne (adv.)—early.
maneo, –ere, –nsi, –nsum—remain.
manifestus, –a, –um—plain, apparent, clear.
manus, –ūs, (f)—hand.
mare, –is, (n)—sea.
margo, –inis, (m)—edge, border.
marītus, –a, –um—married.
marmor, –oris, (m)—marble.
massa, –ae, (f)—lump (of cheese, gold, etc.).
māter, –tris, (f)—mother.
māteria, –ae, (f)—materials, means, opportunity.
mātrōna, –ae, (f)—a married woman, wife.
mātūresco, –ere, –ui—ripen (intrans.).
mātūro, (1)—ripen, hasten (intrans.).
mātūrus, –a, –um—ripe.
maximus, –a, –um—greatest.
medicāmen, –inis, (n)—drug, medicine, remedy.
medicīna, –ae, (f)—medicine.
medius, –a, –um—middle; (with gen.) in the middle of,
    between.
medulla, –ae, (f)—marrow, heart.
mel, mellis, (n)—honey.
membrāna, –ae, (f)—skin, membrane.
membrum, –i, (n)—limb.
memini, –isse (def.)—remember.

memorābilis, -e—remarkable, memorable.
mens, -ntis, (f)—mind.
mensa, -ae, (f)—table.
mensis, -is, (m)—month.
menta, -ae, (f)—mint.
mentior, -iri, -ītus—lie, cheat, deceive.
mereo, and mereor, (2)—deserve.
mergeo, -ere, -si, -sum—immerse, drown.
mergus, -i, (m)—sea-bird, diver.
meritus, -a, -um—deserved, due, proper.
messis, -is, (f)—harvest, crop.
mēta, -ae, (f)—mark, goal.
mētior, -iri, mensus—measure.
metuo, -ere, -ui, -utum—fear, be afraid.
metus, -us, (m)—fear.
mīles, -itis, (m)—soldier.
minimus, -a, -um—smallest, least.
minister, -tṛi, (m)—servant.
minitor (1 dep.)—threaten.
mino, (1)—threaten.
minuo, -ere, -ui, ūtum—diminish, make smaller.
mīrāculum, -i, (n)—marvel.
mīror (1 dep.)—marvel, wonder, admire.
mīrus, -a, -um—wonderful, marvellous.
misceo, -ere, miscui, mixtum—mix.
miser, -era, -erum—wretched, miserable.
miserandus, -a, -um—pitiable.
miseret, (2) (impers.)—pity.
miseror (1 dep.)—pity.
mītis, -e—kind, gentle.
mitto, -ere, mīsi, missum—send.
moderāmen, -inis, (n)—control.
moderātus, -a, -um—moderate, showing moderation.
modo (adv.)—only, just, recently.
modo . . . modo . . .—at one time . . . at another time.
modus, -i, (m)—measure, way, method.

moenia, –ium (n. plur.)—walls.
mōlior (4 dep.)—strive, attempt.
mollesco, –ere—soften, become soft.
mollio, (4)—soften, restrain, make easier.
mollis, –e—soft, tender.
monīle, –is, (n)—necklace.
monimentum, –i, (n)—memorial, monument.
monitus, –ūs, (m)—warning.
mons, –ntis, (m)—mountain.
montānus, –a, –um—of the mountain, dwelling on mountains.
mora, –ae, (f)—delay.
morior, mori, mortuus—die.
mors, –tis, (f)—death.
morsus, –ūs, (m)—bite.
mortālis, –e—mortal, of a mortal man.
mōrum, –i, (n)—blackberry, mulberry.
mōrus, –i, (f)—mulberry-tree.
mōtābilis, –e—moving.
mōto, (1)—move (trans.).
mōtus, –ūs, (m)—movement.
moveo, –ere, mōvi, mōtum—move.
mox (adv.)—soon.
mucro, –ōnis, (m)—sword-point.
mulceo, –ere, –si, –sum—soothe, stroke.
multifidus, –a, –um—split into small pieces.
multum (adv.)—very, most.
multus, –a, –um—much, many.
mundus, –i, (m)—world.
mūnus, –eris, (n)—gift, prize, duty.
murmur, –uris, (n)—murmuring.
murra, –ae, (f)—myrrh.
mūrus, –i, (m)—wall.
mūto, (1)—change, exchange.
mūtus, –a, –um—silent.
mūtuus, –a, –um—mutual, in exchange.

N

nāias, –adis, or nāis, –idis, (f)—water-nymph.
narrātus, –ūs, (m)—story.
narro, (1)—relate, tell a story.
nascor, –i, nātus—be born.
nāta, –ae, (f)—daughter.
nātālis, –e—belonging to one's birth, natal.
nātūra, –ae, (f)—nature.
nātus, –i, (m)—son.
nāvis, –is, (f)—ship.
nebula, –ae, (f)—cloud, mist.
neco, (1)—kill.
nectar, –aris, (n)—drink of the gods; wine.
nego, (1)—deny, refuse.
nemus, –oris, (n)—grove.
nepos, –ōtis, (m)—grandson.
nēquīquam (adv.)—in vain.
nervus, –i, (m)—string (of a lyre).
nescio, (4)—not to know, be ignorant.
nescius, –a, –um—unknowing, unaware.
nex, –cis, (f)—death.
nīdus, –i, (m)—nest.
niger, –gra, –grum—black, dark.
nimis, nimium (adv.)—too much.
nimius, –a, –um—too much, excessive.
niteo, –ere—shine, glitter.
nitidus, –a, –um—shining.
nītor, –i, nīsus, or nixus—strive.
nitor, –ōris, (m)—splendour, lustre.
niveus, –a, –um—snowy, snow-white.
nocens, –ntis—guilty.
noceo, (2), —with dat.—harm.
nocturnus, –a, –um—of the night, nocturnal.
nōmen, –inis, (n)—name, reputation.
nōmino, (1)—call by name.
nondum (adv.)—not yet.

nosco, –ere, nōvi, nōtum—get to know, recognize.
nōtitia, –ae, (f)—knowledge.
noto, (1)—notice, mark.
nōtus, –a, –um (p. part. from nosco)—well-known.
nōvi, (perf. with present sense from nosco)—know, be
    acquainted with.
noviens (adv.)—nine times.
novitas, –tātis, (f)—strangeness.
novo, (1)—renew.
novus, –a, –um—new, recent.
nox, –ctis, (f)—night.
nūbes, –is, (f)—cloud.
nūbilus, –a, –um—clouded, gloomy.
nūbo, –ere, nupsi, nuptum—marry.
nūdo, (1)—make bare.
nūdus, –a, –um—naked, bare.
nullus, –a, –um—no, none.
nūmen, –inis, (n)—divine power.
nurus, –us, (f)—daughter-in-law.
nūto, (1)—nod, wave.
nūtrio, (4)—feed, nurture.
nūtus, –ūs, (m)—nod.
nux, nucis, (f)—nut.
nympha, –ae, (f)—nymph.

O

oblino, –ere, –lēvi, –litum—smear.
oblīquus, –a, –um—crooked, sideways.
oblīviscor, –i, oblītus—forget.
oborior, –oriri, –ortus—arise.
obruo, –ere, –ui, –utum—bury, overwhelm.
obscūrus, –a, –um—dark.
observo, (1)—watch.
obstipesco, –ere, –stipui—be amazed.
obsto, –are, –stiti, –statum—hinder, be in the way of.
obstrepo, –ere, –ui, –itum—shout, make a noise.

obstrūdo, –ere, –si, –sum—force, press down.
obstruo, –ere, –xi, –ctum—stop up, barricade.
obtundo, –ere, –tudi, –tūsum—beat against.
obvius, –a, –um—meeting, in the way.
occāsio, –ōnis, (f)—opportunity, chance.
occāsus, –ūs, (m)—falling, setting (of the sun).
occido, –ere, –cidi, –cāsum—fall, die, fall dead.
occupo, (1)—seize, occupy.
occurro, –ere, –curri, –cursum—meet.
ōcior, –ius—swifter.
oculus, –i, (m)—eye.
ōdi, odisse (def.)—hate.
odōrātus, –a, –um—sweet-smelling, fragrant.
ōlim (adv.)—once, formerly.
ōmen, –inis, (n)—omen.
onus, –eris, (n)—burden.
opācus, –a, –um—dense, thick, shady.
opertus, –a, –um—hidden, covered.
opifer, –era, –erum—bringer of help.
opifex, –icis, (c)—worker, artisan.
oppidum, –i, (n)—town.
ops, opis, (f)—help; (plur.) wealth.
opto, (1)—choose, wish for.
opus, –eris, (n)—work, task.
ōra, –ae, (f)—border, shore, region.
ōrāculum, –i, (n)—oracle.
orbis, –is, (m)—ring, circle, world.
ordior, –iri, orsus—begin.
ordo, –inis, (m)—row, line, series, course.
orgia, –orum (n. plur.)—mystic revels, usually of Bacchus.
orior, –iri, ortus—arise.
orno, (1)—adorn.
ōro, (1)—beg, pray.
orsus, –ūs, (m)—beginning, undertaking.
ortus, –ūs, (m)—rising (esp. of the sun); origin.
ōs, ōris, (n)—mouth, face.

os, ossis, (n)—bone.
osculum, –i, (n)—kiss.
ostendo, –ere, –di, –sum, or –tum—show, display.
ōtium, –i, (n)—leisure.
ōvum, –i, (n)—egg.

P

pabulum, –i, (n)—food, fodder, pasture.
pactum, –i, (n)—agreement.
pactus, –a, –um—settled, agreed upon.
paene (adv.)—almost.
paenitet, (2. impers.)—repent.
palleo, (2)—grow pale, be pale.
pallidus, –a, –um—pale, wan.
palma, –ae, (f)—palm of the hand; palm-tree, date.
palmes, –itis, (m)—tendril, young vine-shoot.
palus, –ūdis, (f)—marsh.
paluster, –tris, –tre—marshy, of the marsh.
pampinus, –i, (m)—a vine-leaf, the foliage of a vine.
pandus, –a, –um—bent, crooked.
par, paris—equal.
paratus, –us, (m)—preparation.
parco, –ere, peperci, parsum—spare.
parens, (c)—father, mother; (plur.) parents.
pāreo, (2)—obey.
paries, –etis, (m)—a wall, usually of a house.
parilis, –e—equal.
pariter (adv.)—equally, like.
paro, (1)—prepare.
pars, partis, (f)—part.
partus, –us, (m)—birth, offspring, bringing forth.
parvus, –a, –um—small.
passim (adv.)—everywhere.
passus, –a, –um—spread out; (of hair) dishevelled.
passus, –us, (m)—a step, pace.
pastor, –oris, (m)—shepherd.

pateo, (2)—be open, lie open, be revealed.
pater, –tris, (m)—father.
paternus, –a, –um—of a father.
patientia, –ae, (f)—patience, endurance.
patior, –i, passus—suffer, endure, allow.
patria, –ae, (f)—native land.
patulus, –a, –um—open, broad, spreading.
paulum, (adv.)—a little, for a little while.
pauper, –eris—poor.
paupertas, –atis, (f)—poverty.
paveo, –ere, pavi—be afraid.
pavidus, –a, –um—afraid, timid.
pecco, (1)—do wrong.
pectus, pectoris, (n)—the breast.
pelagus, –i, (n)—the sea.
pellis, –is, (f)—skin, hide.
pello, –ere, pepuli, pulsum—strike, drive out.
penates, –ium (m plur.)—household gods; house, home.
pendeo, –ere, pependi—hang, hang down.
pendo, –ere, pependi, pensum—pay, weigh.
penitus (adv.)—far within, completely, utterly.
penna, –ae, (f)—feather, wing.
pensum, –i, (n)—spinner's task.
perago, –ere, –ēgi, –actum—pass through, carry out, utter.
percipio, –ere, –cēpi, –ceptum—receive, perceive.
percutio, –ere, –cussi, –cussum—strike; (of a stringed instrument) play.
perdo, –ere, –didi, –ditum—lose, destroy.
peregrīnus, –a, –um—foreign, strange.
pereo, –ire, –ii, –itum—die.
perimo, –ere, –ēmi, –emptum—destroy, kill.
perlūcens, –ntis—transparent.
permātūro, (1)—become quite ripe.
perōsus, –a, –um—hating, detesting, shunning.
perpetuus, –a, –um—unbroken, everlasting.
persequor, –i, –secūtus—follow.

pervenio, –ire, –vēni, –ventum—arrive, reach.
pervius, –a, –um—that can be passed through.
pes, pedis, (m)—foot.
peto, –ere, –ii, –ītum—ask for, seek.
pharetra, –ae, (f)—quiver.
piceus, –a, –um—black as pitch.
pictus, –a, –um—painted, coloured.
piger, –ra, –rum—sluggish, inactive.
piget (me)—it grieves (me).
pignus, –oris, (n)—pledge, pledge of love, child.
pila, –ae, (f)—ball.
pingo, –ere, pinxi, pictum—paint, colour.
pinguis, –e—fat, rich, fertile, greasy.
pinna, –ae, (f)—wing.
pīnus, –i, (f)—pine-tree; ship; pine-torch.
piscis, –is, (m)—fish.
pius, –a, –um—honest, dutiful, pious.
plācātus, –a, –um—peaceful, calm.
placeo, –ere, –ui, –item—please (with dat.).
placidus, –a, –um—calm, peaceful.
plango, –ere, –nxi, –nctum—strike, beat.
plangor, –ōris, (m)—beating, noise, lamentation.
plausus, –ūs, (m)—clapping sound.
plēnus, –a, –um—full, copious; (with gen.) full of.
plūma, –ae, (f)—feather; feather pillow.
plumbum, –i, (n)—lead.
pōculum, –i, (n)—cup, goblet.
poena, –ae, (f)–penalty.
pollens, –ntis—powerful, able.
pollex, –icis, (m)—thumb.
pollicitum, –i, (n)—promise.
polus, –i, (m)—axis, pole, the heavens.
pompa, –ae, (f)—(also plur.) procession.
pōmum, –i, (n)—fruit, generally apple.
pondus, –eris, (n)—weight.
pōno, –ere, posui, positum—put, place, lay aside.

poples, –itis, (m)—knee.
populor (1 dep.)—destroy, lay waste.
populus, –i, (m)—people.
porrigo, –ere, –rexi, –rectum—stretch out.
porta, –ae, (f)—door.
portitor, –ōris, (m)—carrier.
posco, –ere, poposci—demand.
possideo, –ere, –sēdi, –sessum—own, possess.
possum, posse, potui—be able.
posterus, –a, –um—next.
postis, –is, (m)—door-post, door.
postquam (conj.)—after.
potens, –ntis—powerful.
potentia, –ae, (f)—power.
potior (4 dep.)—gain possession of, acquire.
praebeo, (2)—provide, offer, expose, show.
praecēdo, –ere, –cessi, –cessum—go ahead.
praeceps, –cipitis—headlong, rushing, steep, steeply descending.
praecipito, (1)—throw down, rush down.
praecordia, –orum (n. plur.)—breast, heart.
praeda, –ae, (f)—prey, loot.
praedo, –ōnis, (m)—plunderer, robber.
praefero, –ferre, –tuli, –lātum—prefer.
praemium, –i, (n)—prize, reward.
praesāgus, –a, –um—prophesying, presaging.
praesēpe, –i, (n), and praeseps, –is, (f)—stall, pen.
praestans, –ntis—outstanding.
praesuo, –ere, –ui, –ūtum—cover over.
praeter (prep.)—except.
praetereā (adv.)—besides.
praevius, –a, –um—leading the way.
precor (1 dep.)—pray, beg.
prehendo, and prendo, –ere, –di, –sum—grasp.
premo, –ere, pressi, pressum—press, follow.
pretium, –i, (n)—price.

prex, precis, (f)—prayer.
prīmus, –a, –um—first.
priscus, –a, –um—ancient, primitive, antique.
prius (comp. adv.)—previously.
probo, (1)—approve.
proceres, –um (m. plur.)—chiefs.
prōdo, –ere, –didi, –ditum—betray.
prōdūco, –ere, –duxi, –ductum—lead forth; make to grow.
prōfāno, (1)—desecrate, profane.
proficiscor, –i, profectus—set out.
profundum, –i, (n)—sea.
profundus, –a, –um—deep.
prōgenies, –ei, (f)—offspring, progeny.
prohibeo, (2)—prevent.
prōles, –is, (f)—offspring, descendant.
prōmitto, –ere, –mīsi, –missum—promise.
prōmo, –ere, prompsi, promptum—take out.
pronepos, –ōtis, (m)—great-grandson.
prōnus, –a, –um—bending forward, going downward.
propero, (1)—hurry, hasten.
prōpositum, –i, (n)—plan, intention.
prospicio, –ere, –spexi, –spectum—look forward to, look out
    for, see.
prōsum, prōdesse, prōfui—be of use, benefit.
prōtinus (adv.)—immediately.
pruīnōsus, –a, –um—frosty.
prūnum, –i, (n)—plum.
pudor, –ōris, (m)—shame.
puella, –ae, (f)—girl.
puellāris, –e—girlish.
puer, –i, (m)—boy.
puerīlis, –e—boyish.
pullus, –a, –um—black, dark-coloured.
pulso, (1)—beat, strike.
pulvis, –eris, (m)—dust.
purpura, –ae, (f)—purple cloth.

purpureus, –a, –um—purple.
pūrus, –a, –um—pure, unadulterated.
puto, (1)—think.

Q

quā (adv.)—where.
quadriiugi, –orum (m. plur.)—a four-horse team.
quadripes, –pedis—having four feet.
quaero, –ere, quaesīvi, quaesītum—seek, ask for.
quam (adv.)—than.
quantus, –a, –um—how great.
quartus, –a, –um—fourth.
quater (adv.)—four times.
quatio, –ere, (no perf.), quassum—shake.
quercus, –ūs, (f)—oak-tree.
querella, –ae, (f)—complaint, plaintive noise.
queror, –i, questus—complain.
questus, –ūs, (m)—complaint.
quīcumque, quaecumque, quodcumque—whoever.
quisque, quaeque, quodque—each one.
quisquam, quicquam—anyone, anything (after negative).
quō (adv.)—to where.
quondam (adv.)—formerly.
quoniam (conj.)—since, because.
quoque (conj.)—also.
quotiens (conj.)—whenever.

R

radio, (1)—gleam.
radius, –i, (m)—ray (of the sun).
rādix, –icis, (f)—root, radish.
rādo, –ere, –si, –sum—shave, scrape, scratch.
rāmālia, –ium (n. plur.)—twigs, branches.
rāmus, –i, (m)—branch.
rapidus, –a, –um—swift.
rapīna, –ae, (f)—theft.

rapio, –ere, –ui, raptum—seize, carry off.
rapto, (1)—steal, carry away.
raptor, –ōris, (m)—robber, abductor.
rastrum, –i, (n)—rake.
ratio, –ōnis, (f)—thought, plan, reason, way, method.
raucus, –a, –um—hoarse, harsh.
recens, –ntis—fresh, new.
recido, –ere, –cidi, –cāsum—fall back.
recipio, –ere, –cēpi, –ceptum—receive.
recondo, –ere, –didi, –ditum—hide; (oculos) close again.
rector, –ōris, (m)—helmsman, driver, ruler.
rectus, –a, –um—straight.
reddo, –ere, –didi, –ditum—give back, utter.
redimīculum, –i, (n)—necklace, fillet.
redoleo, (2)—smell, give off a scent.
refero, –ferre, –tuli, –latum—bring back; tell (a story).
refugio, –ere, –fūgi—shrink from.
refugus, –a, –um—fleeing.
regero, –ere, –gessi, –gestum—throw back.
regio, –ōnis, (f)—district.
rēgius, –a, –um—royal.
regno, (1)—rule.
regnum, –i, (n)—kingdom.
relābor, –i, –lapsus—slip back.
relego, –ere, –lēgi, –lectum—collect again.
relevo, (1)—relieve, rest.
relinquo, –ere, –līqui, –lictum—leave, abandon.
remaneo, –ere, –si, –sum—remain.
rēmigium, –i, (n)—oar.
remissus, –a, –um—loose, slack.
remitto, –ere, –mīsi, –missum—let go, abandon.
remollesco, –ere—grow soft again.
remoror (1 dep.)—delay, linger.
removeo, –ere, –movi, –motum—remove.
renīdens, –ntis—shining.
repāgulum, –i, (n)—bar, bolt.

repello, –ere, reppuli, repulsum—drive back.
repenté (adv.)—suddenly.
reperio, –ire, repperi, repertum—find.
repetītus, –a, –um—(as adv.) repeatedly, again and again.
repeto, –ere, –ii, –ītum—seek again.
repleo, –ere, –plēvi, –plētum—refill.
repōno, –ere, –posui, –positum—put aside.
repperio—see reperio.
repugno, (1)—oppose.
requies, –ētis, (f)—rest, respite.
requiesco, –ere, –ēvi, –ētum—rest, repose.
requiro, –ere, –sīvi, –sītum—ask for, inquire.
reseco, –are, –ui, –sectum—cut off.
resisto, –ere, –stiti—resist, remain.
respicio, –ere, –spexi, –spectum—look back.
respondeo, –ere, –di, –nsum—reply.
restitvo, –ere, –vi, –utum—restore.
resto, –are, –stiti—remain.
resupīnus, –a, –um—on one's back, lying flat.
retego, –ere, –xi, –ctum—uncover.
retexo, –ere, –xui, –xtum—weave anew.
reticeo, –ere, –ui—remain silent.
retineo, –ere, –ui, –entum—keep, hold back.
retracto, (1)—feel again.
retrō (adv.)—backwards.
revello, –ere, –velli, –vulsum—tear away.
reverentia, –ae, (f)—respect, awe.
revoco, (1)—call back.
revolvo, –ere, –volvi, –volūtum—roll over.
rictus, –ūs, (m)—open mouth.
rigeo, –ere—be stiff, stiffen.
rigesco, –ere, –ui—grow hard; stand on end (hair).
rigidus, –a, –um—stiff.
rigor, –ōris, (n)—numbness, hardness.
riguus, –a, –um—well-watered.
rīma, –ae, (f)—cleft, chink.
rīpa, –ae, (f)—bank of a river.

rogo, (1)—ask.
rogus, –i, (m)—funeral pile, pyre.
rōrans, –ntis—dewy, dripping.
rostrum, –i, (n)—beak, muzzle, snout.
rota, –ae, (f)—wheel.
rubeo, –ere—be red.
rubesco, –ere, –ui—grow red.
rubēta, –orum (n. plur.)—bramble-thickets.
rubor, –ōris, (m)—redness.
rudis, –e—rough, common, untaught.
rūgōsus, –a, –um—wrinkled, shrivelled.
rūmor, –ōris, (m)—rumour.
ruo, –ere, rui, rutum—rush.
rūpes, –is, (f)—rock.
rūricola, –ae, (c)—living in the country, rustic.
rursus (adv.)—again.
rusticus, –a, –um—belonging to the country, rustic.
rutilus, –a, –um—golden, ruddy.

S

sacer, –cra, –crum—holy.
sacerdos, –dōtis, (c)—priest, priestess.
sacra, –orum (n. plur.)—sacrifice, holy rites.
sacro, (1)—consecrate.
saeculum, –i, (n)—lifetime, generation, age.
saepe (adv.)—often.
saevus, –a, –um—savage, cruel.
sagitta, –ae, (f)—arrow.
sagittifer, –era, –erum—bearing arrows.
salio, –ire, –ui—leap, dance; (of a vein) pulse.
saltem (adv.)—at least.
saltus, –ūs, (m)—leap, mountain-pass.
salūs, –ūtis, (f)—safety.
sānābilis, –e—curable.
sanctus, –a, –um—holy.
sanguineus, –a, –um—bloody.

sanguis, –inis, (m)—blood, offspring.
sapiens, –ntis—wise.
satur, –ura, –urum—sated, full of food.
satus, –a, –um—son of, sprung from.
saucius, –a, –um—wounded, hurt.
saxeus, –a, –um—stone, turned to stone.
saxum, –i, (n)—rock, stone.
scelerātus, –a, –um—wicked, impious.
scindo, –ere, –scidi, scissum—split, rend asunder.
scio, (4)—know.
scītor, (1 dep.)—seek to know, inquire.
scrobis, –is, (m)—hole, ditch.
sculpo, –ere, –psi, –ptum—carve.
sēcēdo, –ere, –cessi, –cessum—withdraw.
seco, –are, –ui, sectum—cut.
secundus, –a, –um—second, favourable.
secundae mensae—second course.
sēcūrus, –a, –um—safe, free from care.
sedeo, –ere, sēdi, sessum—sit.
sēdes, –is, (f)—seat, home, dwelling-place.
sedīle, –is, (n)—chair.
sēdūco, –ere, –xi, –ctum—draw, aside, set aside.
sēdulus, –a, –um—busy.
seges, –itis, (f)—crop (of corn, etc.)
sēmen, –inis, (n)—seed.
semper (adv.)—always.
senex, senis, (m)—old man.
senīlis, –e—of or belonging to old people, aged.
senior, –oris, (m)—elder.
sententia, –ae, (f)—opinion, view.
sentio, –ire, sensi, sensum—feel.
sentis, –is, (f)—thorn, brier.
septem (indecl.)—seven.
sepulcrum, –i, (n)—tomb.
sepultus, –a, –um—buried.
sequor, –i, secūtus—follow.

sera, –ae, (f)—bolt of a door.
serēnus, –a, –um—cloudless, fair, bright.
sērius (comp. adv.)—later.
sermo, –ōnis, (m)—speech, words, conversation.
sero, –ere, sēvi, satum—sow.
sero, –ere, –rui, sertum—weave, entwine.
serpens, –ntis, (m)—snake.
serta, –orum (n. plur.)—garlands.
sērus, –a, –um—late.
servio, (4)—serve (with dat.)
servo, (1)—save, preserve.
setius (adv.)—otherwise.
sicco, (1)—dry.
siccus, –a, –um—dry.
sīdus, –eris, (n)—star; season, weather.
signo, (1)—mark, seal.
signum, –i, (n)—signal, sign.
silens, –ntis—silent.
silentium, –i, (n)—silence.
silex, –icis, (m)—pebble.
silva, –ae, (f)—wood.
similis, –e—like, similar.
simplex, –icis—simple, innocent.
simul (adv.)—together, at the same time.
simulac—as soon as.
simulācrum, –i, (n)—image, phantom.
simulo, (1)—imitate, copy.
sincērus, –a, –um—real, pure, genuine.
sine (prep.)—without.
singuli, –ae, –a—separate, individual.
sino, –ere, sīvi, sītum—permit, allow.
sinus, –ūs, (m)—curve, fold, lap, bosom.
sisto, –ere, stiti, –statum—set up, place, stop.
sitis, –is, (f)—thirst.
situs, –a, –um—situated, placed.
socio, (1)—associate, accompany.

socius, –i, (m)—comrade; (with gen.) associate in.
sōl, sōlis, (m)—sun.
solidus, –a, –um—solid.
solitus, –a, –um—usual, accustomed.
sollemne, –is, (n)—solemn rite, religious festival.
sollicitus, –a, –um—anxious, disturbed.
solum, –i, (n)—ground, soil, land, region.
sōlus, –a, –um—alone, single.
solvo, –ere, –vi, –ūtum—loosen, set free, discharge.
sonans, –ntis—noisy, resounding.
sonitus, –ūs, (m)—noise, sound.
sonus, –i, (m)—noise, sound.
sordidus, –a, –um—dirty, sooty.
soror, –ōris, (f)—sister.
sors, sortis, (f)—lot, condition, luck.
spargo, –ere, –rsi, –rsum—scatter.
spatior (1 dep.)—walk about, travel.
spatium, –i, (n)—space, distance, course.
species, –ēi, (f)—appearance, shape.
speciōsus, –a, –um—beautiful.
spectaculum, –i, (n)—show.
spectātor, –ōris, (m)—spectator.
specto, (1)—look at, see.
specus, –us, (m)—cave.
sperno, –ere, sprēvi, sprētum—despise.
splendidus, –a, –um—shining, brilliant.
sponte sua—of his, its, own accord.
spūmiger, –era, –erum—foaming.
spūmo, (1)—foam.
squālidus, –a, –um—dirty.
squāma, –ae, (f)—scale.
stagnum, –i, (n)—pool, swamp.
stāmen, –inis, (n)—warp, (vertical thread) of a loom.
statuo, –ere, –ui, –ūtum—establish, decide.
stella, –ae, (f)—star.
stillo, (1)—drip, trickle; (trans.) drop, let fall.

stimulus, –i, (m)—goad.
stīpes, –itis, (m)—log, trunk of a tree.
stipula, –ae, (f)—stalk.
stīva, –ae, (f)—plough-handle.
sto, stare, steti, statum—stand.
stolidus, –a, –um—dull, stupid.
strāmen, –inis, (n)—straw, thatch.
strāta, –orum (n. plur.)—bed-coverings, bed.
strīdeo, and strīdo, –ere, –di—hiss.
strīdor, –ōris, (m)—noise.
strīdulus, –a, –um—hissing, whistling.
stringo, –ere, –nxi, –ictum—touch lightly, graze; draw (a sword).
stupeo, –ere, –ui—be astonished.
subeo, –ire, –ii, –itum—approach, spring up under.
subiectus, –a, –um—lying near to.
subitō (adv.)—suddenly.
submoveo, –ere, –mōvi, –mōtum—remove, keep away.
succēdo, –ere, –cessi, –cessum—approach (with dat.)
succendo, –ere, –di, –sum—set fire to, kindle.
succresco, –ere—be supplied anew.
succutio, –ere, –ussi, –ussum—fling aloft.
sūcus, –i, (m)—juice, moisture.
sūdor, –ōris, (m)—sweat, secretion.
sufficio, –ere, –fēci, –fectum—be enough.
summissus, –a, –um—low.
summum, –i, (n)—top, surface.
summus, –a, –um—highest, topmost.
sūmo, –ere, sumpsi, sumptum—take, wear.
super (prep. with acc.)—above.
      (adv.)—on top, thereupon.
superi, –orum (m. plur.)—the gods.
supero, (1)—overcome.
supersum, –esse, –fui—survive; (with abl.) survive from.
superus, –a, –um—upper; of the upper world.
supīnus, –a, –um—lying on the back, thrown backwards.

suppleo, –ere, –vi, –etum—fill up, complete.
supplex, –icis—suppliant.
surgo, –ere, surrexi, surrectum—rise.
sūs, suis, (c)—pig.
suscito, (1)—arouse.
suspirium, –i, (n)—sigh.
sustineo, –ere, –tinui, –tentum—hold up; tolerate, bear;
   (with dat.) resist.

T

tābesco, –ere, –ui—melt away, decay.
tacitus, –a, –um—silent.
taeda, –ae, (f)—pinewood, pine-torch, marriage-torch.
tālāria, –ium (n. plur.)—ankles.
tālus, –i, (m)—heel.
tamen (conj.)—however.
tamquam (adv.)—as if.
tango, –ere, tetigi, tactum—touch.
tantum (adv.)—so much, only.
tantus, –a, –um—so great.
tardus, –a, –um—slow.
tectum, –i, (n)—roof, house, building.
tego, –ere, –xi, –ctum—cover, conceal.
tegumen, tegminis, (n)—covering, shield.
tēla, –ae, (f)—web, loom.
tellus, –uris, (f)—land, earth.
tēlum, –i, (n)—weapon.
temerārius, –a, –um—rash, daring.
tempestīvus, –a, –um—timely, opportune.
templum, –i, (n)—temple.
tempora, –um (n. plur.)—the temples of the head.
tempto, (1)—try, feel.
tendo, –ere, tetendi, tensum, or tentum—stretch out, ex-
   tend, travel.
tenebrae, –arum (f. plur.)—darkness.
teneo, –ere, –ui, tentum—hold, keep, keep in control.

tener, –era, –erum—soft, tender.

tenuis, –e—thin, weak.

tenuo, (1)—draw out, make thin.

tepeo, –ere—be warm.

tepidus, –a, –um—lukewarm, cooled.

ter (adv.)—three times.

teres, –etis—rounded, polished, smooth.

tergeo, –ere, tersi, tersum—wipe clean.

tergum, –i, (n)—back.

tergus, –oris, (n)—back, side.

terni, –ae, –a—three.

terra, –ae, (f)—land, earth.

terreo, (2)—frighten.

terribilis, –e—dreadful, terrifying.

tertius, –a, –um—third.

testa, –ae, (f)—brick, tile.

textus, –a, –um—woven, plaited together.

thalamus, –i, (m)—marriage.

thyrsus, –i, (m)—an ivy-wreathed staff, carried by Bacchus
or his worshippers.

tiāra, –ae, (f)—turban.

tībia, –ae, (f)—pipe, flute.

tignum, –i, (n)— log, beam.

timeo, (2)—fear.

timidus, –a, –um—frightened, subject to fear.

timor, –ōris, (m)—fear.

tingo, –ere, –nxi, –nctum—colour, dye, wet.

tinnulus, –a, –um—clashing, tinkling.

titulus, –i, (m)—honour, title.

tollo, –ere, sustuli, sublātum—raise, remove.

tonsus, –a, –um—cropped, shaven.

torpor, –ōris, (m)—numbness.

torqueo, –ere, torsi, tortum—twist.

torreo, –ere, –ui, tostum—bake, roast.

tortus, –a, –um—crooked, twisted.

torus, –i, (m)—couch.

(170)

totidem (indecl.)—the same number of, just as many.
tōtus, -a, -um—whole, entire, total.
tracto, (1)—touch, handle.
tractus, -ūs, (m)—trail, track, course.
traho, -ere, traxi, tractum—pull, draw.
traiicio, -ere, -iēci, iectum—transfix.
trāmes, -itis, (m)—footpath.
transeo, -ire, -ii, -itum—cross.
transitus, -ūs, (m)—a means of crossing.
tremebundus, -a, -um—quivering, shaking.
tremo, -ere, -ui—shake, shiver, tremble.
tremulus, -a, -um—quivering, trembling.
trepidans, -ntis—fearful.
trepido, (1)—be in a state of alarm.
trepidus, -a, -um—fearful.
trēs, tria—three.
tribulus, -i, (m)—a kind of thorn or thistle.
trifidus, -a, -um—three-pronged, divided into three.
tristis, -e—sad.
trīticeus, -a, -un—of wheat, made of wheat.
trītus, -a, -um—worn, rubbed.
triumphus, -i, (m)—a triumphant procession.
trunco, (1)—cut off, strip.
truncus, -i, (m)—tree-trunk.
tuba, -ae, (f)—trumpet.
tueor, -eri—watch over.
tumulo, (1)—bury.
tumulus, -i, (m)—mound, grave.
tunica, -ae, (f)—tunic.
turba, -ae, (f)—crowd, throng.
turbo, (1)—disturb, agitate.
turpis, -e—shameful.
turris, -is, (f)—tower; a dovecote in the form of a tower.
tūs, tūris, (n)—incense.
tūtēla, -ae, (f)—protection.
tūtus, -a, -um—safe.

tympanum, –i, (n)—drum.
tyrannus, –i, (m)—ruler, despot.
tyrius, –a, –um—Tyrian, purple.

U

ūber, –eris—rich, fruitful.
ūdus, –a, –um—wet, moist.
ulna, –ae, (f)—arm.
ultimus, –a, –um—last, furthest.
ultra (adv.)—further, longer; (prep. with acc.) beyond.
ululo, (1)—howl, shriek.
umbra, –ae, (f)—shadow, shade, ghost.
umerus, –i, (m)—shoulder.
ūmidus, –a, –um—damp, wet.
unda, –ae, (f)—wave, water; (plur.) water.
unde (adv.)—whence.
undique (adv.)—everywhere.
unguis, –is, (m)—nail, claw.
ūnicus, –a, –um—one, single, sole.
ūnus, –a, –um—one, alone.
urbs, –bis, (f)—city.
urgeo, –ere, ursi—press, press on with, drive.
urna, –ae, (f)—urn, water-jar.
ūro, –ere, ussi, ustum—burn (trans.)
usque (adv.)—continually.
ūsus, –ūs, (m)—use, experience, enjoyment.
ut, uti (conj.)—(with indic.) as, when; (with subj.) in order
    that.
uterque, utraque, utrumque—each (of two).
ūtilis, –e—useful.
utinam (adv.)—would that.
ūtor, –i, ūsus—use, treat (with abl.).
utrimque (adv.)—on both sides, on either side.
ūva, –ae, (f)—grape.

V

vaco, (1)—be empty; (with abl.) be free from.

vacuus, –a, –um—empty; unemployed; (with abl. or gen.)
free from, empty of.

vado, –ere—go.

vagor (1 dep.)—wander.

vale!—farewell!

valeo, (2)—be strong, healthy; have influence; (with inf.)
be able to.

vallis, –is, (f)—valley.

vānus, –a, –um—vain, useless.

vastus, –a, –um—immense, vast.

vāticinor (1 dep.)—foretell, prophesy.

vātes, –is, (m)—priest, prophet.

vēlāmen, –inis, (n)—covering, garment, cloak, veil.

vellus, –eris, (n)—fleece.

vēlo, (1)—cover, deck.

vēlox, –cis—swift.

vēlum, –i, (n)—veil; sail.

vēna, –ae, (f)—vein (of blood or metal).

venēnum, –i, (n)—poison.

venia, –ae, (f)—pardon.

ventus, –i, (m)—wind.

vēr, vēris, (n)—the spring.

verbum, –i, (n)—word.

vereor (2 dep.)—fear.

verro, –ere, verri, versum—sweep.

verso, (1)—turn, twirl.

vertex, –icis, (m)—head, top, whirlpool.

verto, –ere, –ti, –sum—turn, change.

vērus, –a, –um—true.

vesper, –eris, and –eri, (m)—evening.

vestigium, –i, (n)—foot, footprint, trace.

vestis, –is, (f)—garment.

veto, –are, –ui, –itum—forbid.

vetus, –eris—old.

via, –ae, (f)—way, road.
vibro, (1)—make to shake.
vicem, –is, (no nom., f)—change, turn, alternation.
in vicem, in vices—in turn.
vīcīnia, –ae, (f)—neighbourhood, proximity.
vīcīnus, –a, –um—neighbouring, near, (with dat.).
victor, –oris, (m)—and victrix, –icis, (f)—conqueror.
video, –ere, vīdi, vīsum—see.
vīlis, –e—cheap, worthless.
villa, –ae, (f)—country-house, farm.
villōsus, –a, –um—hairy, shaggy.
villus, –i, (m)—shaggy hair.
vīmen, –inis, (n)—twig.
vincio, –ire, –nxi, –nctum—bind.
vinco, –ere, vīci, victum—conquer.
vinculum, –i, (n)—chain, rope.
vindex, –icis, (m)—avenger, defender.
vīnum, –i, (n)—wine.
viola, –ae, (f)—violet.
vīpereus, –a, –um—of a snake.
vir, viri, (m)—man, husband.
virens, –ntis—green, flowering.
viresco, –ere—grow green.
virga, –ae, (f)—twig, branch.
virgineus, –a, –um—girlish.
virgo, –inis, (f)—girl.
viridis, –e—green.
vīs, (no gen.), plur. vires, (f)—force, power.
viscus, –eris, (n)—usually plur.—internal organs.
vīso, –ere, –si, –sum—look at, visit.
vitio, (1)—make faulty, spoil, infect.
vitis, –is, (f)—grape-vine.
vitium, –i, (n)—fault, defect, vice.
vīto, (1)—avoid.
vitta, –ae, (f)—ribbon, head-band.
vīvo, –ere, vixi, victum—live.

vīvus, –a, –um—living, alive.
vix (adv.)—scarcely.
vōcālis, –e—singing, vocal.
voco, (1)—call.
volātus, –ūs, (m)—flight.
volo, velle, volui—wish, be willing.
volvo, –ere, volvi, volūtum—turn, roll along, make to fall.
volucer, –cris, –cre—swift-flying.
volūmen, –inis, (n)—coil, fold.
voluntas, –tātis, (f)—will, wish, disposition, goodwill.
vōmer, –eris, (m)—ploughshare.
vomo, –ere, –ui, –itum—pour forth.
vōtum, –i, (n)—prayer.
voveo, –ere, –i, vōtum—wish for.
vox, vōcis, (f)—voice, words.
vulgāris, –e—commonly known.
vulgo, (1)—make known everywhere, publish.
vulnus, –eris, (n)—wound.
vultus, –ūs, (m)—face, look.

Z

zephyrus, –i, (m)—breeze.
zōna, –ae, (f)—belt, girdle.